HEAVEN
HELP
US ALL

Christian Spiritual Growth

ELDER: ERROL GORDON SR.

WESTBOW
PRESS®
A DIVISION OF THOMAS NELSON
& ZONDERVAN

This book is a work of non-fiction. Unless otherwise noted, the author and the publisher make no explicit guarantees as to the accuracy of the information contained in this book and in some cases, names of people and places have been altered to protect their privacy.

WestBow Press books may be ordered through booksellers or by contacting:

WestBow Press
A Division of Thomas Nelson & Zondervan
1663 Liberty Drive
Bloomington, IN 47403
www.westbowpress.com
844-714-3454

Because of the dynamic nature of the Internet, any web addresses or links contained in this book may have changed since publication and may no longer be valid. The views expressed in this work are solely those of the author and do not necessarily reflect the views of the publisher, and the publisher hereby disclaims any responsibility for them.

Any people depicted in stock imagery provided by Getty Images are models, and such images are being used for illustrative purposes only. Certain stock imagery © Getty Images.

Scripture taken from the King James Version of the Bible.

ISBN: 978-1-6642-6536-3 (sc)
ISBN: 978-1-6642-6535-6 (hc)
ISBN: 978-1-6642-6537-0 (e)

Library of Congress Control Number: 2022908082

Print information available on the last page.

WestBow Press rev. date: 05/11/2022

Introduction

Heaven helps us all is a plea of Humanity worldwide, some more than others. Without the help from our Heavenly Father in Heaven, His Son Christ Jesus, the divine power of the Holy Spirit that Jesus sent back to us with the permission of the Father, and the faithful, obedient angels that Jehovah God uses to do his will. We would probably not be here now in this generation.

We, the people of the earth, need all the help we can get from Heaven in these troublesome times that we are living. To our loving Heavenly Father, be Glory, Honor, and praise always and forever for loving us so much that He sent His only Son, Jesus the Christ, to be used as the lamb of God in taking away the sins of the world. And Jesus gives all those that followed him and live a righteous life, with the help of the Holy Spirit, the hope of everlasting life with Him in Heaven.

This book is divinely inspired to help all who will read the detailed and understandable information therein to seek more of Jesus, who is the only way to God's Kingdom. My prayer is that the help and blessings that we all need from Heaven to survive in these turbulent times with our families will continuously be poured down. My desire is to inspire, encourage, motivate, rejuvenate, educate, and pray for spiritual increase for us all.

Seek first the Kingdom of God before trying to store up all your hard-earned treasures here on this earth where it is going to be left behind when our name is called up yonder for our spiritual transitioning. My sisters and brothers in Christ, and everyone else who will allow their hearts to welcome Jesus in their lives, do what is right in the eyes of God, who sees and knows all things. May he continue to bless you and your family in Jesus's Name; I pray, Amen.

Elder: Errol Gordon Sr.

Contents

1

Don't Stress the Test of the Enemy

In your hands is a tremendous resource of inspired revelations written upon the foundation of the Bible. So throughout this book, *Heaven Help Us All,* you will discover many quoted scriptures from the King James Version of the Bible. These scriptures are spiritual nourishment that we all need to stay on the right path that leads to God's kingdom. Inspiration, encouragement, gratitude, discoveries, and realizations that will remind us that our dependency is on the heavenly host to help us in these turbulent and troublesome times. Please enjoy your reading, and may God continue to bless you and your family in Jesus's name. Amen.

Suppose you are a born-again spiritual child of God, that truly love our loving Creator. And, of course, you know then that you are in the army of the Lord. (Then please do not stress the test.) Our Lord and Savior Jesus Christ knows all his sheep. And Satan also knows that you are not one of his followers living by the sinful desires of the flesh and doing evil deeds to please him. Therefore, you are going to be unknowingly on his list to be recruited through Satan's well-known, cunning tactics and temptations. We are living now in the days when many biblical prophesies are being fulfilled, signs that undoubtedly demonstrate that God's enemy is close to being bound.

The Bible refers to him as a roaring lion going about seeing whom he can devour. The Bible also informs us that Satan is here to steal, kill, and destroy. And so as God's children are surrounded by evil deeds on every side, they are feeling like what King David experienced when he said, "Although I walk through the valley of the shadow of death I will fear no evil for thou art with me thy rod and thy staff will comfort me."

We, the children of the Most High God, have put all our faith and trust in our loving heavenly Father, which has relieved us of the overburdened stress the world's people are feeling. Brothers and sisters, the pressure is on, and only the spiritually strong will survive the evil wrath these last days will bring.

> This know also, that in the last days perilous times shall come. For men shall be lovers of their own selves, covetous, boasters, proud, blasphemers, disobedient to parents, unthankful, unholy, Without natural affection, trucebreakers, false accusers, incontinent, fierce, despisers of those that are good, Traitors, heady, highminded, lovers of pleasures more than lovers of God; Having a form of Godliness, but denying the power thereof: from such turn away. (2 Timothy 3:1–5)

All these things mentioned in the reading are seen around us. Children are killing their own parents. We are also told the following in 2 Timothy 2:15–16, "Study to show thyself approved unto God, a workman that needeth not to be ashamed, rightly dividing the word of truth. But shun profane and vain babblings: for they will increase unto more ungodliness."

God himself inspired the Bible, allowing for the telling of some of his creation stories like the experience of his beloved son's visitation to earth through the miraculous birth of a virgin. His work, death, and resurrection bring him back home. So through the working of his Holy Spirit, God helps humanity understand his love, grace, and mercy and helps us follow a righteous journey in life.

The tremendous knowledge we get from studying the words of God and the wisdom of our loving heavenly Father will give us our understanding. It allows us to always call upon the all-powerful name of Jesus when we feel any stress because the evil one will not win. The enemy knows about the Bible because he quoted scriptures, even to Jesus. And he knows what the Bible said in Galatians 5:22–26.

> But the fruit of the Spirit is love, joy, peace, longsuffering, gentleness, goodness, faith, meekness, temperance: against such there is no law. And they that are Christ's have crucified the flesh with the affections and lusts. If we live in the Spirit, let us also walk in the Spirit. Let us not be desirous of vain glory, provoking one another, envying one another.

As children of God who walk in the Spirit, we will be tested on each of these individual fruits of the Spirit. We have to function differently from the people of the world, and it is said, "By the fruit you shall know them." Jesus was tested in the wilderness because Satan was out to prove that Jesus was who he said he was. Now we are tested on whether we possess love.

For example, imagine your niece did you wrong long before you were born again in Christ. It's likely the communication between you two ended. But once you began growing in the Spirit, it was set up that you bumped into each other at the mall. Will you show her that you love her by hugging her? If you had changed in your inner spirit from who you used to be and hugged her, she would instantly realize that something was different about you. Then you could explain that you are now a Christian, which could encourage her to visit your church and probably get saved.

Joy

You are being tested on whether joy is growing in you now. Before you were born again, the pressure of the world was heavy on your heart. You would usually get mad very quickly while being tested. For example, imagine you are walking into the house with two bags of groceries you just bought at the store. You trip on the step, both bags fall, and everything gets destroyed, including the eggs. Instead of fussing and cussing, a song you heard at church comes up through your spirit. Then you call your son to come and help you clean things up. He may be thinking to himself, *Is this my same mother?* And because of the change he sees in you, he begins to show you more respect.

Peace

Maybe your job accidentally shorted you by two days' pay. You peacefully go to your manager and show him your pay stub in a quiet way, in a way you would have never done before you became a Christian. Because of the excellence of your approach, he apologizes and then asks, "Are you okay? I haven't known you to be this calm about your money."

Then you can explain that you have found Jesus and are not the same person you used to be. This could inspire him to make changes for himself, like going back to church.

Long-suffering

Imagine your daughter brings over her three children for you to watch on Friday morning and says she would be back to get them by 5:00 p.m. the same day. It so happens that you are being tested and do not know.

Something happens with her, so she does not come back to get the children until Wednesday. For six days, you have to suffer from the noise, and the mess becomes unbearable. When she comes to get them, she prepares herself for how upset she thought you would be. But she sees the opposite.

She asks, "Are you okay, Mom? This is not like you. Jesus has truly changed you from who you used to be."

And you smile and say, "Yes, my daughter, but don't push your luck."

Gentleness

The people across the street ask you, "Are you okay? Why are you so kind and mild-mannered, letting your neighbor get away with what he is doing to you with his evil self? How can you tolerate this unruly neighbor disrespecting you and saying the things he just did?"

And you only reply, "Everything is going to be all right."

"You are not the person I used to know. You would have taken him on. Now you are cutting the grass outside his gate along with yours. Why?"

They do not know that it was the testing of the enemy to see your reaction, but now you've proven to the evil one that Jesus is working in your life and you have had a spiritual rebirth and it feels terrific. Three days later, the neighbor knocks on your front door and apologizes and says he will not disrespect you again. So you invite him to church the next Sunday, and he goes.

Goodness

What exactly is goodness? The word *good* is used so frequently in our everyday lives that it's almost lost its meaning. But the Bible tells us that the word *good* actually means holy, pure, and righteous. Goodness is godliness and can often be seen in our actions when

5

our hearts are pure. Our God is a good God. It's not just what he does; it's who he is. In Psalm 46, the psalmist says that God is our refuge and strength, a present help in times of trouble, and this is why we can say with absolute confidence that God is good. To us as Christians, goodness involves righteousness, or doing what is right.

Goodness is often viewed as kindness, but it is deeper than that, spiritually speaking. For example, one day your neighbor says, "I always see you giving food to that old man living down the street. You seem to get along with everyone around here."

You reply, "I am a Christian. My goal is to be with Jesus one day in heaven, and I have to follow Jesus and live a godly life to get there. My hands have to be clean of evil doings, and my heart has to be pure. So it feels good inside for me to get along with everybody and help anyone I can."

Faith

The enemy of God and humans will also test the faith of anyone who professes to be a Christian and pretends they are walking by faith. Hebrew 11:1 reads, "Now faith is the substance of things hoped for, the evidence of things not seen." For example, the phone rings, and your niece is calling to tell you that her husband has been shot and is in the hospital. She asks you to pray for him.

You get down on your knees and pray and ask God not to let him die, and in your heart, you truly believe that God is going to answer your prayers and save him. The next day she calls back and says that the doctor said the bullet missed his vital organs and he is going to be ok.

All you could say is, "To God be the glory forever."

All of the spiritual fruits mentioned so far are daily principles of living as a Christian. The life of a Christian is not just a weekend exercise. It is a day-and-night living experience, and our enemy knows that. He has a lot of tricks in his bag to try to reflect our focus on other seemingly important matters that, spiritually speaking, were not as important as what was in your heart concerning the ministry. As Christians, we have to prioritize our daily schedule to include space and time for the things of God.

The enemy takes pleasure in letting us not believe in ourselves if we allow him to do so and that we are growing with a balanced diet of spiritual nourishment intake. That will produce the outcome that everyone can see, observe, and know we are not who we used to be. Instead we are functioning in a different and better way that can be described as spiritual fruits. We also have to always remember that we are not standing on our own might or accomplishing these godly endeavors by our individual expertise or professionalism, but understand that none of these accomplishments would be possible if it were not for the power of the Holy Spirit working with our inner spirit.

We also need to be conscious that no one soldier is encouraged to go into battle as a loner; instead there are others to support each individual's efforts. As Christian soldiers in the army of the Lord warring against the spiritual enemy, we have to exercise the spiritual fruit called love, be very quick in our responsive support of each other, and help one another in encouragement and all additional help that our sisters or brothers might need from time to time. It is suitable for every Christian soldier to have close prayer partners or spiritual friends that can be called on anytime, day or night, for spiritual support if needed. Our godly love of each other should be a lot stronger than even the sometimes phony love of the world. So many people use the word *love* for their selfish gain and twisted motives.

It is an excellent thing to have someone or more than one person to even reflect on scriptures that the pastor might have shared in the Sunday sermon. The more your heart chews on spiritual nourishment, the more digestive it will be for your inner spirit. Matthew 18:20 says, "For where two or three are gathered together in my name, there am I in the midst of them." Christians should always have something godly on their hearts, even throughout the working day, since we all are multitalented and can multitask.

Once you become a follower of Christ, the enemy will always have an eye on you or assign one of his demons to monitor your everyday movements. The Holy Spirit keeps them at bay, but their influence is not always something you can trample under your feet. However, with the help of the Holy Spirit, we will not stress their test because we were not given the spirit of fear, and we have the utmost confidence in the power of the Holy Spirit so we are totally dependent and assured.

To keep from stressing the devilish test of the enemy, we should remember the inspired words of the apostle Paul in Romans 8:31–32, "What shall we then say to these things? If God be for us, who can be against us? He that spared not his own Son, but delivered him up for us all, how shall he not with him also freely give us all things."

Christians have to understand the depth of God's love for us all, especially the people who have earnestly become followers of his loving Son, Christ Jesus. Everything on God's side of the equation is good and perfect; the issues are on our human's sinful and born-again side of the equation. We truly have to study to show ourselves approved, and with the help of the Holy Spirit, we will be able to stand firm in these evil days.

To keep from stressing the test of God's enemy and ours also who are children of God, reading and studying the inspired words of God in the Bible is our lifeline. We have to be vigilant and determined in our hearts and inner spirit that no matter what might come our way, we will be strong in our faith and do as the apostle Paul in his determination to carry on his ministry. Romans 8:35–39 reads,

> Who shall separate us from the love of Christ? Shall tribulation, or distress, or persecution, or famine, or nakedness or peril, or sword? As it is written, for thy sake we are killed all the day long; we are accounted as sheep for the slaughter. Nay, in all these things

we are more than conquerors through him that
loved us. For I am persuaded, that neither death,
nor life, nor angels, nor principalities, nor powers,
nor things present, nor things to come, Nor height,
nor depth, nor any other creature, shall be able to
separate us from the love of God, which is in Christ
Jesus our Lord.

When I am inspired to write to all Christians worldwide and say
we will not stress the test of the enemy of God and us, it is because
I will also inform everyone that there are other lifestyles and godly
living that I know will be needed in order to declare without a doubt
that we will not stress the test. Again, for the convenience of all
readers, I have quoted all scriptures from the King James Version of
the Bible in my writing.

So that whether you are at the beach; traveling by plane, train, or
in the passenger seat or back seat of your form of transportation for a
vacation to the mountain or valleys below; or even relaxing at home,
when I make mention of scripture in your reading, you do not need
to reach for the Bible or wait until you get home to see for yourself
the words of the Bible in the quoted scriptures. To God be the glory.

As I often make mention of studying the words of God to show
ourselves approved, the main reason is that the Bible was inspired
with everything we need for our journey to everlasting life in God's
kingdom. And many Christian sisters and brothers cannot seem to
find the time necessary to feast on the written words of God for
the spiritual nourishment we all need. The enemy is very good at
keeping people away from the scriptures because he knows he will
have less chance of tricking you into believing that what seems
wrong is not truly that bad.

He will generate reasons that it is only how you look at what he
would have you do whether it is better to do it in the daytime than
at night. The enemy is very cunning, and he is good at twisting the
understanding of what is right or wrong. As far as we are concerned

as Christians, no question would be asked if the Bible said it is wrong to do a particular deed. It is wrong.

So with all of that explanation, I will now allow us to read from the Bible. Romans 12:1–21 reads,

> I BESEECH you therefore, brethren, by the mercies of God, that ye present your bodies a living sacrifice, holy, acceptable unto God, which is your reasonable service. And be not conformed to this world: but be ye transformed by the renewing of your mind, that ye may prove what that good is, and acceptable, and perfect, will of God. For I say, through the grace given unto me, to every man that is among you, not to think of himself more highly than he ought to think; but to think soberly, according to as God hath dealt to every man the measure of faith.

> For as we have many members in one body, and all members have not the same office: So we, being many, are one body in Christ, and every one members one of another. Having then gifts differing according to the grace that is given to us, whether prophecy, let us prophesy according to the proportion of faith; Or ministry, let us wait on our ministering: or he that teacheth, on teaching; Or he that exhorteth, on exhortation: he that giveth, let him do it with simplicity; he that ruleth, with diligence; he that showeth mercy, with cheerfulness.

> Let love be without dissimulation. Abhor that which is evil; cleave to that which is good. Be kindly affectioned one to another with brotherly love; in honor preferring one another; Not slothful in business; fervent in Spirit; serving the Lord;

Rejoicing in hope; patient in tribulation; continuing instant in prayer; Distributing to the necessity of saints; given to hospitality.

Bless them which persecute you: bless, and curse not. Rejoice with them that do rejoice, and weep with them that weep. Be of the same mind one toward another. Mind not high things, but condescend to men of low estate. Be not wise in your own conceits. Recompense to no man evil for evil. Provide things honest in the sight of all men. If it be posible, as much as lieth in you, live peaceably with all men. Dearly beloved, avenge not yourselves, but rather give place unto wrath: for it is written, Vengeance is mine; I will repay, saith the Lord. Therefore if thine enemy hunger, feed him; if he thirst, give him drink: for in so doing thou shalt heap coals of fire on his head. Be not overcome of evil, but overcome evil with good.

I hope and pray that everyone does understand that every word that has been read is an action needed for us to answer the question, "What would Jesus do?" The written words of the Bible are our sword for this spiritual warfare that we are pressing our way through to victory in Jesus. The Holy Spirit is our administrator and the one that assigns godly functions and kingdom work needing to be done. There is no need for jealousy in the body of Christ. If you are chosen for a particular assignment, the Holy Spirit will intertwine with your inner spirit to let you feel your appointment.

Your internal spiritual connection will communicate with your heart, and the heaviness you will feel will push you in the direction you are called to do much-needed kingdom work. Do not fight the feeling. Be reminded of Jonah, who knew what his assignment was, and try to fight the emotions and urging of the Spirit. As we have heard, Jonah decided to go his own way and was brought back the hard way.

The more we as Christians are dedicated to the knowledge of God and the ministry of the kingdom, the less time we will have to entertain negative vibes from the enemy who always want to sow bad seed among the excellent source of our heavenly Father. We have to really think about ourselves and know just who we are. For instance, let us visit 1 Corinthians 3:16–21.

> Know ye not that ye are the temple of God, and that the Spirit of God dwelleth in you? If any man defile the Temple of God, him shall God destroy; for the temple of God is holy, which temple ye are. Let no man deceive himself. If any man among you seemeth to be wise in this world, let him become a fool, that he may be wise. For the wisdom of this world is foolishness with God. For it is written, He taketh the wise in their own craftiness. And again, The Lord knoweth the thoughts of the wise, that they are vain. Therefore let no man glory in men. For all things are yours.

Sometimes when I read the words of God, a fatherly feeling comes over me because I get the feeling that our loving God inspired his words to truly help humans whom he really loves with all his heart. I feel the specialness of the love that our God has shown to the man and woman that he made in his own likeness. And what a blessing to know that the almighty God and Creator would choose to allow the Holy Spirit to dwell and commune with our inner God-given inner spirit. The enemy knows these things, and the jealousy he possesses, with his understanding of the interaction and closeness that we have and can be multiplied to become even closer to our God and Creator, is driving him straight to the pit of fire.

Oftentimes people do not stop to think of themselves as the temple of God. I have seen people who were maybe just churchgoers rather than Christians smoking cigarettes outside of a church, putting all that harmful smoke into the temple of God right there in the churchyard. We have to even be careful of what we eat or be more mindful of eating in moderation.

Another important thing that we as Christians must observe and pay some attention to understand is the world's wisdom. The more wisdom and spiritual growth we get from our heavenly Father, the more humble we should be. In other words, the godly man full of wisdom should be full of humility and be the most humble in the room. The world *action* is the opposite because the more knowledge they get, the more big-headed they become, thinking they are wise. God gives wisdom. That is why I can understand why a lot of people with good education get themselves in trouble.

They have the knowledge that is learned, but no wisdom to use and control the learning. As Christians, we have to keep our minds from going astray on not kingdom-worthy thoughts. The apostle Paul encouraged the Philippian Christians in the same manner. In Philippians 4:8, Paul wrote, "Finally, brethren, whatsoever things are true, whatsoever things are honest, whatsoever things are just, whatsoever things are pure, whatsoever things are lovely, whatsoever things are of good report; if there be any virtue, and if there be any praise, think on these things."

The Spirit of God and the knowledge of the Bible allow us, children of God, to declare that we will not stress the test of the enemy. The enemy will try to let our minds wander on many ungodly ventures. Like someone listening to a radio station and the next segment of broadcasting is not welcome, that person just has to turn the dial to another station. Likewise, when the evil one tries to lock our thoughts on sinful ideas, we have to train ourselves to switch our thinking to something pure or of good report.

The Bible helps us to understand that God did not give us a spirit of fear. So the enemy does not control us in any way or form.

He just likes to share what sometimes seems like good suggestions that, in the end, if we allow it to take root in our heart, will lead us to do something wrong or will be pleasing to the evil one. God is the only one that we, as children of God, desire to please. It is not good to eat from two tables at the same time.

Every child of God known as a Christian does have a testimony of God's love and his goodness, saving grace, provision, protection, deliverance, and guidance. And many will testify that it was only the blessings of God that they are here today to testify before you how God helped them up from the terrible state they were experiencing.

Preaching one Sunday during his sermon, a pastor delivered a heartfelt, attention-grabbing testimony of how he was only eight years clean and sober from drugs and alcohol abuse. He really allowed others to reflect on their selves as he explained how he was so strung out back in the days before the Mothers Against Drunk Driving (MADD) venture and the new speed limit came into existence.

I heard others say that they did not know how they reached home because of how drunk they were. This pastor's testimony was eye-opening for the congregation because he spoke from his heart to let them understand that he was not always what he is now. To prove the power of God's savings grace and how blessed we are that Jesus came when he did and to be so good to us that on his return to his heavenly Father, he sent the Holy Spirit to build the church from where he left off.

So for many people, when this ungodly enemy of God tries to get them to return to what they used to be, they rebuke him openly because as good as the corn and watermelon were in Egypt, no one in their right mind would want to go back into that backbreaking slavery. So why does Satan think that with the blood of Jesus, we are saved from slavery sins? And as good as the parties and other sinful ventures were, does he think we desire to go back to the sinful bondage we were all in up to our lifeline?

Maybe he does since many others had yielded to his crafty temptations and backslid to what they used to do before they were saved. The Bible lets us know that at the time when the blood of Jesus saved us. The Holy Spirit entered within us that all the other devilish, demonic spirit had to flee. Still, it gave us the understanding that because of our desires and sinful actions, the Holy Spirit left because he will not tarry in an unholy vessel. When he departed, those other evil spirits that were there before you were born again will return and bring a lot more of their family members and friends with them.

So a personal note to the enemy: we are not going to be afraid of your tests and temptations because we have been there and have already done those things you keep repeating to humans. Now you are not using snakes anymore. Instead you are using our family, friends, coworkers, and neighbors to lead us into the broad and spacious road. Our God, through his inspired word, the Bible, has already told us that many do find it, and this spacious road is going to lead a lot of people to destruction.

Get behind us, Satan. You were Lucifer, son of the morning. And because of your hateful spirit and jealous attitude, you were taken down from the high office you once enjoyed. And just like the innocent snake you used in the garden of Eden, you were also put low, crawling around. You never gave up your evil ways and will soon be bound for a thousand years and, then after that, your final destruction. So get behind us, children of the Most High God.

Sisters and brothers, young and older, let us tighten up our armor and leave no loose part untightened because our enemy is looking for a loose linkage. If it is so wiggles, he thinks it just might break and he then can steal our attention. Our loving heavenly Father has given us a new heart and renewed our inner spirit so that good deeds we did not think we were capable of having become easy for us to do in the view of the astonishing microscope of many who are focused on our actions now that we are Christians rather than asking God to save their souls.

Another pastor in his sermon testified of his changed heart as he told the story of how when he was a little boy, a man came to their house and killed his mother and sister and was sent to prison. For so many years, he was so full of rage, but as the years went by, God blessed him to grow up, save his soul, and allow him to become a member of the spiritual army of Christ. He said it came into his heart one day to visit that same man who had killed his mother and sister. And he said he did and preached Jesus's saving grace to him.

This born-again newness of the heart is a very riveting testimony of a renewed inner spirit. When we become daughters and sons of God and are led by the Holy Spirit of God to do what is good and right in our loving heavenly Father's eyes, we all should live our daily lives to achieve this honor, glory, and praise to him for which we always will be blessed.

2

Peace of Mind: A Priceless Commodity

When we think of the word *peace*, Jesus using this same word when he calmed the storm on the ocean probably come to our minds when he said, "Peace be still." Let us read this story from the source. Mark 4:35–41 reads,

> And the same day, when the even was come, he saith unto them, Let us pass over unto the other side. And when they had sent away the multitude, they took him even as he was in the ship. And there were also with him other little ships. And there arose a great storm of wind, and the waves beat into the ship, so that it was now full.
>
> And he was in the hinder part of the ship, asleep on a pillow: and they awake him, and say unto

him, Master, carest thou not that we perish? And he arose, and rebuked the wind, and said unto the sea, peace be still. And the wind ceased, and there was a great calm. And he said unto them, Why are ye so fearful? how is it that ye have no faith? And they feared exceedingly, and said one to another, What manner of man is this, that even the wind and the sea obey him?

When I say "peace of mind," it simply means that I know that the tremendous power of God through the working of the Holy Spirit can and does bring peace to troubled minds worldwide. Can you take a moment to imagine? Jesus spoke directly to the storm and the sea, and the wind obeyed him as if they had hearing and understanding in their existence. That is why, my sisters and brothers, we can rest assured that if we continue trusting and putting all our faith in Jesus.

He would speak directly to our minds so burdened with the struggle it takes to survive in this troublesome world. And the hearts and minds of all God's people will listen to him, which will result in peace of mind. Many people might look at first and think that money would bring all the peace required in our life journey, but it is well noted that even rich people commit suicide because of problems generated from troubled minds.

Jesus is the master of giving peace of mind. We can totally depend on him through faith in the kingdom of God. We humans will not be able to generate enough faith to acquire peace of mind by ourselves without the help of the Holy Spirit who was sent here on earth to help us by the heavenly powers of God. "Heaven helps us all" is a statement that should be understood.

All Jesus's sheep know and will always work to let the world understand that heaven is where God, his Son, Christ Jesus, and all the spiritual hosts of God reside. And God from his throne in heaven has been sending blessings down to us even before he blew the breath of life into the two first humans, allowing them to become living souls. We looked to heaven from which comes all our help to make it through the turbulent waters of life.

Through faith in God, we can take many actions to help ourselves with maintaining our peace of mind when we receive it. The first thing we all need to be mindful of has been recorded in the scripture, which plainly tells us that the enemy of God is here among us to steal, kill, and destroy. Satan and his demons are going about seeing whose peace of mind they can steal or disturb, with the hope of destroying your peace. Let us reflect on 1 Peter 5:6–11.

> Humble yourselves therefore under the mighty hand of God, that he may exalt you in due time: Casting all your care upon him; for he careth for you. Be sober, be vigilant; because your adversary the devil, as a roaring lion, walketh about, seeking whom he may devour: Whom resist stedfast in the faith, knowing that the same afflictions are accomplished in your brethren that are in the world. But the God of all grace, who hath called us unto his eternal Glory by Christ Jesus, after that ye have suffered a while, make you perfect, stablish, strengthen, settle you. To him be Glory and dominion for ever and ever. Amen.

As Christians and children of God through the blood of Christ Jesus, we have to wrap our heads around the fact that God the Father has done so much more than what we deserve. God the Son has done so much more than what we deserve, and God the Holy Spirit is doing so much more than we deserve. The heavenly host has prepared everything that humans needed to one day depart the bondage of the sinful flesh and join them in the spiritual realm so far away from this evil, wicked, and troublesome existence we are in now. Everything is in place for us, and we have to understand

and do our part in this godly process. It seems that our trust, faith, confidence, and dependability are not accumulating to the point of where they should be since we asked Jesus Christ to come in and be the ruler in our lives.

Being born again and growing as new spiritual children of God, it is essential that each of these four characteristics is being prayed for and that we are willing not to allow the destructive influence of the ruler of this world with all his cunning antics to deter us from our heavenly commitment. We are too caught up in the things of this world, the lovely home, which of course is good. The adorable dependable cars for which we get our family and us where we need to be are also good. Emergency money in our bank accounts to withstand whatever comes out of the woodwork at us is perfect. Lots of technology apparatus for all the family, including security for the home, is lovely.

Many good families and friends for moral support, if needed, are excellent. And all the other delightful and enjoyable things that keep us smiling since it is much better to be happy than to be sad are complementary. Brothers and sisters, God desires for us to live a good and productive life as he blessed us, so please do not think that all the things mentioned are not things we should all have. I hope you notice that, of all the things mentioned, nothing spiritual was among them.

I include scriptures quotes in this book because the whole reason for this book is to help us all or even some of us as God's children to be inspired, encouraged, and enlightened, to reflect on ourselves as to where we are in Christ, to monitor our individual spiritual growth, and to shed a constant light on the narrow road that will lead us all to God's kingdom. In the Bible, Jesus uses the idea of seed metaphorically in more than one parable to explain how different people receive the word of God.

In Matthew 13:24–30, Jesus painted a picture of two sowings that I would like all the readers to be conscious of because even as I write these statements, the same conditions are happening without the attention of many. In the midst of good living with very good intentions, other little ungodly things can creep into our lives without being noticed if we are not careful.

Let us reflect on Matthew 13:24–28.

> Another parable put he forth unto them, saying, The Kingdom of Heaven is likened unto a man which sowed good seed in his field: But while men slept, his enemy came and sowed tares among the wheat, and went his way. But when the blade was sprung up, and brought forth fruit, then appeared the tares also. So the servants of the householder came and said unto him, Sir, didst not thou sow good seed in thy field? From whence then hath it tares? He said unto them, An enemy hath done this.

The point being made here is that in our lives as Christians, we have to be knowledgeable of the fact that in the midst of all the good life we are trying to live, the enemy of God will sow bad seeds that we are not mindful of or paying attention to, which is sinful when we align the action with the word of God.

When we visit Colossians 3:1–10, we will understand that there are many things the children of God have to guard against from being a part of our lives. It reads,

> If Ye then be risen with Christ, seek those things which are above, where Christ sitteth on the right hand of God. Set your affection on things above, not on things on the Earth. For ye are dead, and your life is hidden with Christ in God. When Christ, who is our life, shall appear, then shall ye also appear with Him in Glory.

Mortify therefore your members which are upon the Earth; fornication, uncleaness, inordinate affection, evil concupiscence, and covetousness, which is idolatry: For which things sake the wrath of God cometh on the children of disobedience: In which ye also walked some time, when ye lived in them. But now ye also put off all these; anger, wrath, malice, blasphemy, filthy communication out of your mouth. Lie not one to another, seeing that ye have put off the old man with his deeds; And have put on the new man, which is renewed in knowledge after the image of him that created him:

Put on therefore, as the elect of God, holy and beloved, bowels of mercies, kindness, humbleness of mind, meekness, longsuffering; Forbearing one another, and forgiving one another, if any man have a quarrel against any: even as Christ forgave you, so also do ye. And above all these things put on charity, which is the bond of perfectness. And let the Peace of God rule in your hearts, to the which also ye are called in one body; and be ye thankful. Let the word of Christ dwell in you richly in all wisdom; teaching and admonishing one another in psalms and hymns and spiritual songs, singing with grace in your hearts to the Lord. And whatsoever ye do in word or deed, do all in the name of the Lord Jesus, giving thanks to God and the Father by him.

If you have just taken the time to read the Bible quotes, please bear in mind that this book is written specifically for Christians worldwide. If you have not been born-again and are walking in the newness of your spiritual rebirth, these scriptures can step on many toes. As Christians, we understand that we have to store up our treasures in heaven and not pile up our all in all on this earth. Peace comes from God, and the closer we are with him, the easier it will be to get and retain peace of mind.

Suppose you are reading this book and have not given your life entirely to God through his Son Jesus. In that case, I will take this opportunity to encourage you to attend a church service, and they will answer any question you might have and be willing to help you turn your life over to Jesus. Please do it before it is too late. Thank you.

In this troubled world we are living in, evil is running rampant. It is challenging for true Christians to keep the spiritual armor on, do everything that is required of them, and work and pay the bills necessary for living a decent life. Walking as it might feel sometime in the valley of the shadow of death and through their faith and trust in the heavenly Father, they feel no fear and concentrate on their spiritual health at the same time. It is then even more difficult for the people who have not given their lives to Jesus and walk by faith to cope in these troublesome times.

Many have turned to drugs and alcohol to help them with peace of mind that is never found where they are trying to obtain it. There is a lot of suffering worldwide, and no one individual has the perfect answer or solution to the world's problems. We know as Christ-followers that we put all our burden at his feet and walk by faith one day at a time because without faith, it is impossible to please God. We must keep our focus on the fact that these evil days will not be extended too much longer for God to make a change since we believe that we are living at the end of time.

We as Christians also know that we will have our share of tribulations, sickness, pain, and sometimes little or no money to do all that needs to be done, but yet through the grace of God, we stand firm for his glory. God is bringing peace of mind to many troubling situations in every country around the world. He is providing food, articles of clothing, houses, and shelters for many through other people who can afford to give and organizations working for the kingdom of God because he is a great provider from even before the beginning of time for humans. God provides the need, not the wants, as King David said in the book of Psalm, "The Lord is my shepherd I shall not want."

Sometimes many people complain that the glass is half-empty instead of seeing it as half-full and giving thanks to God. The peace of a troubled mind can be right there next to negative thoughts and not getting noticed because of the way many people are thinking. My version of the serenity prayer can be a blessing to all of us in helping to generate dependency on the one that spoke peace to the windy storm on the ocean, as it stated,

> Heavenly Father, the God of all creation, through your Son Christ Jesus and the working power of your Holy Spirit, please give me the serenity to accept without reservation and stress the things that are not in my power to understand or change. Please bless me with the courage and determination to do, accomplish, and change whatever is in my power to change. And please, oh my God of all wisdom, grant me the knowledge, wisdom, and understanding to leave the other things that are hurting humanity that I cannot understand in your mighty hands.

Some humans have a very weak tendency to try to solve their problems, and by doing so, they end up with even more problems, like a man in a new city who decided he was not going to ask anybody for any direction. He did not want to tell his wife that he had forgotten his cell phone at home and had no technology to help him. He wanted to let his family think that he knew where he was going, and because of his foolish pride and ego, he kept driving his wife and three children.

They needed to use the bathroom so badly that the baby had peed on himself in the car. He kept going around, sometimes repeating the same turns. His wife was the one who asked the driver beside them as they stopped at the red light for direction and found out where they were going. The man had just needed to make two right turns instead of the left turns he kept making. Then he got very upset with the baby boy for peeing in the car.

Often many of us make the same type of misjudgment by not going to God in prayer for direction in our decision-making. Unfortunately we make a mess of ourselves with stress and anxiety because we were not putting our dependency on God. For God to lead us in the way we need to go, we have to believe that he can and will work things out for us because through his Holy Spirit, a message could be quickly sent to our inner spirit on which way to proceed. The Bible said it is not even in our strength to direct our steps.

So many mistakes have been made throughout most of our lives. We do not need to wonder about what God is going to do. Our loving heavenly Father has already established everything for us from the beginning of time. We as people tend to concentrate on what God has done, what he is doing now, and what he will do in the future, even in the very beautiful. Gospel songs we listen to are all about the functioning of God and his blessings on us humans. Not much is being said about human behavior and what we should do to please our heavenly provider. As Christians, many things are going unnoticed by many in their conduct and faithfulness to our Creator.

In Colossians 3, we read the apostle Paul was and is still trying to let Christians then and now be reminded that if we are genuinely committed to the fact that we are renewed and risen with Christ, we have to think differently from the former days when we were in slavery to sin. Before, most of our attention probably was on just making it the best we can in this world. Getting a good education for those so blessed and privileged, many people worldwide with less than the average education will still receive eternal life in God's kingdom, only by being born again, keeping clean hands, and being pure in their hearts, living godly, satisfying lives.

Paul made it plain that we as Christians have to begin to seek heavenly endeavors. He explains that our affection has to be now set on things above and not on only things that satisfy us here on earth. He reminds us that on the day of baptism when we went down under the water, we were dead at that point to the old life, and when we arose, our new life now is hidden with Christ in God. That is why we are called new creatures.

Now my sisters and brothers, young and older, now we have to do what we have to do. Remember, we are talking about peace of mind that only God can give us. And this peace of mind has a lot to do with our lifestyle, conduct, and functioning. Many things for self-pleasure that we used to enjoy doing in the past life before we were saved by God's grace now have to be thrown out in the trash for dumping far away from our lives. The Bible is very specific about immoral conduct, which is easily and often used by Satan to entice people into doing wrong.

And so, we are encouraged to mortify the many members of our body that are being used for temptation. One of the main things is fornication, which means having sex without being married. Every Sunday, there are many people worldwide in churches living and sleeping with someone and having sex without a ring on the finger, which is called "shacking up." Many other conducts will keep us out of the kingdom of God and block our peace that could not find itself in our minds because of our disturbed conscience.

The new person we are supposed to become should be renewed in knowledge after his image that created us, being able to put on as the elect of God, holy and beloved, bowels of mercies, kindness, humbleness of mind, meekness, and long-suffering. And let us not forget godly love among one another, something I have seen lacking in many churches I once was a part of. I have tried to work to defuse tensions and generate peace in the house of the Lord. I have witnessed one family that did not want to associate or speak with another family in the same church because of misunderstandings they had in the past. And choir members have difficulty speaking to each other and even try to avoid looking at each other.

Let it be known that all these conducts mentioned can rob us of our peace of mind. The Bible speaks about anger, wrath, malice, blasphemy, and filthy communication out of our mouths. It admonishes us not to lie to one another and says we should be forbearing and forgiving one another. The Bible said we should let the peace of God rule in our hearts because we are called in one body. We should be thankful, and whatsoever we do in our words or deeds, we should do it all in the name of the Lord Jesus, giving thanks to God and the Father by him.

Songs are always more about what God is doing and will do for us. In my personal opinion, I think that many people would appreciate some songs that do remind them of Christians living and the things we need to do to please our loving heavenly Father. The fruits of the Spirit would probably be suitable for a lovely song. Hopefully, I will hear it from a singer who read this book. From the day that God said that all of his creation was good, the benefits to his beloved humans were in writing and his heart.

The love of God for us began on the day he was inspired to create us in his own image and likeness. His only begotten Son, Christ Jesus, who came down and gave his life for our free-will decision-making that went totally wrong, is a testament of the heavenly love they have surrounding us here on earth. God specifically had spoken to King Solomon, the son of King David, and told him concerning the Israelites then, which goes for us now as well, the words recorded in 2 Chronicles 7:14, "If my people, which are called by my name, shall humble themselves, and pray, and seek my face, and turn from their wicked ways; then will I hear from Heaven, and will forgive their sin, and will heal their land."

Here we are in an even better position because Jesus took care of the sin by giving us a spiritual rebirth to free us from that sin bondage. Yet people are still allowing the enemy of God to influence them with his cunning self in wrongdoings. The enemy only gives suggestions, as he did with Jesus in the wilderness. He cannot put anyone's hands on something wrong or pick anyone up and put them in a bed with another married person to commit adultery. Neither can he compel anyone to hate their sisters or brothers before he gives them something to eat. No, he cannot and does not. He is good at stealing peace of mind by enticing the weaker part of us all if we allowed him to do so. He knows Jesus had to be hungry when he suggested the stone-into-bread temptation. But Jesus quickly rebuked him. "Man shall not live by bread alone," he was told.

In like manner, we have to be ready to promptly rebuke him as well when he approaches us with enticing suggestions. For example, a married Christian man is driving down a street and sees a beautiful lady walking a block away from where he needs to turn. Still, this man's attention gets the best of him. He drives around two blocks because it is a one-way street to come back in the lovely-shape lady direction to ask if she needs a ride, all with lustful desires in his heart.

However, innocent as it might seem and the goodwill the man thinks he is doing, Satan knows he has a weakness for the next temptation. Even that kindness could be turned into a disastrous situation when Satan finishes working his magic with both of them riding in the car. One mistake or a wrong decision can ruin the peace of mind mentality that we are working so hard to achieve. Many family relationships are destroyed, and many children grow up with one or no parents because of decisions made that were not in the family's best interest. "Lead me not into temptation and deliver me from all evil" was David's prayer, which we can also include in our prayers. Satan is working more to destroy Christians who are not grounded in the words of God.

However, we ought to remember that many times the traps and schemes of Satan to corner us and mess us up are turned into good by God through his Holy Spirit. If it were not for God protecting us from the evil one, we would not be able to smile or enjoy any peace of mind. Glory be to our heavenly Father for his love, grace, and mercy. To maintain peace and tranquility in our lives, we need to always remember that we have a God above any problem or situation we will encounter. We can always depend on a loving God to answer our prayers and stretch out his hands to retrieve us when we fall into the troublesome waters of life.

There are so many hurting people worldwide, encountering one trying situation after another and sometimes multiple problems at the same time. High blood pressure, diabetes, and many other sicknesses are on the rise, and many are caused by stress and a lack of peace of mind. Many people who were not believers are now facing the reality that we might be living at the end of time, although new buildings are being built all the time and twenty years or more plans have been put on the table for future projects. There are also the concerns of children being born every day somewhere in the world.

Through the shed blood of his Son Jesus and the working power of the Holy Spirit, God is the only one that will be able to keep our hearts and minds in a peaceful state. Because the peace of God is not controlled by anyone born on this planet, it is not sold in any stores or cannot be purchased with cash or credit cards. If humans could sell this godly peace of mind, it would probably be the most expensive commodity on the stock market. And then we think how easy it is for anyone to partake of it by just aligning ourselves with God. The message is clear why some people have more peace of mind than others.

The words of God said, "For he himself is our peace, who has made us both one and has broken down the dividing wall of hostility in his flesh. And the peace of God, which surpasses all understanding, will guard your hearts and your minds in Christ Jesus." Now may the Lord of Peace himself give you peace at all times in every way.

Many scriptures will bring the comfort of peace to the people of God. Philippians 4:7 reads, "And the Peace of God, which passeth all understanding, shall keep your hearts and minds through Christ Jesus." A very long time ago, before Jesus came to earth, the Hebrew prophet Isaiah, who was born in Jerusalem and lived about seven hundred years before the birth of Christ, prophesied between 701 and 740 B.O. concerning Jesus's birth and called him the Prince of

Peace. Isaiah 9:6 reads, "For unto us a child is born, unto us a son is given: and the government shall be upon his shoulder: and his name shall be called Wonderful, Counsellor, The mighty God, The everlasting Father, The Prince of Peace."

This prophet was truly a man of God, full of the Spirit, and blessed with many revelations. He prophesied with a strong determination and gave his people much encouraging information on relying on and trusting in their God. Let us read together Isaiah 26:2–4, "Open ye the gates, that the righteous nation which keepeth the truth may enter in. Thou will keep him in perfect peace, whose mind is stayed on thee: because he trusteth in thee. Trust ye in the Lord forever: for in the Lord JEHOVAH is everlasting strength."

Brothers and sisters in Christ, by encouraging people everywhere, I am also encouraging myself. As Christians, this means we are following Jesus. As he said, "Come follow me, and I will make you a fisher of men."

We have to remember that peace is one of the fruits of the Spirit, Galatians 5:22. And also in Matthew 5:9, Jesus himself let us understand that the peace-makers will be blessed. And in Luke 28:36, after Jesus's resurrection, as the disciples were in conversation, Jesus stood in the midst of them and said, "Peace be unto you."

Although Jesus is now at the right hand of our heavenly Father, he will never forget any of his promises to his followers. On the very last day before Jesus went home to heaven from which he came, he blessed his disciples, whose blessings are extended even to us here in these turbulent times. Everything Jesus said to them then includes all followers until he comes for his church.

Let us read what happened on the day he returned home. Luke 24:45–52 states,

> Then opened he their understanding, that they
> might understand the scriptures, And said unto
> them, Thus it is written, and thus it behooved
> Christ to suffer, and to rise from the dead the third

day: And that repentance and remission of sons should be preached in his name among all nations, beginning at Jerusalem. And ye are witnesses of these things. And behold, I send the promise of my Father upon you: but tarry ye in the city of Jerusalem, until ye be endued with power from on high.

And he led them out as far as to Bethany, and he lifted up his hands, and blessed them. And it came to pass, while he blessed them, he was parted from them and carried up into Heaven, And they worshipped him and returned to Jerusalem with great joy: And were continually in the temple, praising and blessing God. Amen.

The disciples stayed in Jerusalem, and on the day of Pentecost, the promise did come to them and us now because they could not have made it without the Holy Spirit, and neither can we now in these troublesome times. With the help of the Holy Spirit, we all are encouraged in Romans 12:18, "If it be possible, as much as lieth in you, live peaceable with all men." The apostle Paul went on to encourage us even more in 2 Corinthians 13:11, "Finally, brethren, farewell. Be perfect, be of good comfort, be of one mind, live in peace; and the God of love and peace shall be with you."

And so the prayer for heaven to bless and help us all is very sincere. And through faith, the one thing we should not be without or leave home without, it has to be cherished, protected, increased, and nourished to be able to exercise our faith always in God, through his Son, Christ Jesus, with the continued help of the Holy Spirit. Keep our hearts and minds focused intently on the hope that is before us, to be in the heavenly kingdom with the one we are following, our Lord and Savior, Jesus Christ. To our heavenly Father be all the glory, honor, and praise forever. Amen. God is always good.

3

*Jesus at the Right Hand of
His Heavenly Father*

To God be the glory forever. "Who is at the right hand of the
Father?" someone might ask. And the answer is "Jesus." That is
correct. Over one hundred Bible scriptures testify to this fact in the
Old and New Testaments. Jesus came from heaven to earth because
of the love of the Father to redeem humanity from the destruction
of sin that was upon each one born on Planet Earth. The Bible made
it clear in John 1:1–5,

> In the beginning was the Word, and the Word was
> with God, and the Word was God. The same was in
> the beginning with God. All things were made by
> him; and without him was not any thing made that
> was made. In him was life; and the life was light of

men. And the light shineth in darkness; and the darkness comprehended it not.

We all know that Jesus is the one that came and died on the cross for all humanity. But at no time did he ever make any statement that he was on his own in doing this tremendous life-saving endeavor. He specifically made it clear that he was doing his heavenly Father's will. When he was asked to teach the disciples how to pray, he says in Matthew 6:9–13,

> After this manner, therefore, pray ye: Our Father which art in Heaven, Hallowed be thy name. Thy Kingdom come. Thy will be done in Earth, as it is in Heaven. Give us this day our daily bread. And forgive us our debts, as we forgive our debtors. And lead us not into temptation, but deliver us from evil: For thine is the Kingdom, and the power, and the Glory, for ever. Amen.

Here in this prayer, Jesus is teaching us how to pray to the Father. And because Jesus declares he is the door and no one can go to the Father without him, at the end of our prayer, we say, "in the name of Jesus." Jesus is not waiting at the right hand of his Father to take over the throne. First of all, our heavenly Father will never die as humans do. The Father is God, the Supreme Being, the Creator. Our God is omnipotent, omniscient, and omnipresent. And he is omnibenevolent, and he has eternal existence. Jesus has no intention of overthrowing his Father like King David's son, Absalom, or Adonijah, who plotted to sit on his father's throne because his father, David, was now old and ready to give up the throne. Jesus is not trying to take his Father's throne, and he wants us to always go to his Father in his name.

However, there is a division between churches preaching and how some allow their congregation to address Jesus as God, praying and only glorifying Jesus. Jesus desires all praise to go to God the Father, unlike God's enemy, Satan, who had to be cast out of heaven because of the jealousy he had of the praises and glory going to God the Father. All churches should be on one accord since we are all followers of Jesus in giving God the Father all the honor, glory, and praises that he alone deserves. When we pray, we should direct our prayers to God the Father in the name of his Son, Christ Jesus. Nothing will get done until the Father gives the Son the ok and Jesus then gives the Holy Spirit the green light to carry out the Father's wishes.

God the Father was the one that said to the others, "Let us make man in our image and likeness," and so here we are, existing under the umbrella of the Trinity, God the Father, God the Son, and God the Holy Spirit, three different entities with one purpose and representing only one God. And is told in Psalm 83:18, "That men may know that thou whose name alone is JEHOVAH, art the most high over all the earth."

Never pray only to Jesus or Jesus's earthly mother. Direct your prayers to God the Father through his only begotten Son, Jesus, and you will get divine results. The Father sent Jesus to earth, and when Jesus returned to the Father, Jesus sent the Holy Spirit to us with the approval and blessing of the Father.

The apostle Peter gave the most eloquent sermon on the day of Pentecost when the Holy Spirit came to us in that upper room. Because of the misunderstanding it brought into the city that day, Jesus's disciples being in the Spirit were thought to be drunk early in the morning. So Peter, with the help of the Holy Spirit, had to explain to the gathering crowd what was taking place. Acts 2:29–34 reads,

> Men and brethren, let me freely speak unto you of the patriarch David, that he is both dead and buried, and his sepulcher is with us unto this day. Therefore being a prophet, and knowing that God

had sworn with an oath to him, that of the fruit of
his loins, according to the flesh, he would raise up
Christ to sit on his throne; He seeing before this
before spake of the resurrection of Christ, that his
soul was not left in hell, neither his flesh did see
corruption. This Jesus hath God raised up, whereof
we all are witnesses. Therefore being by the right
hand of God exalted, and having received of the
Father the promise of the Holy Ghost, he hath shed
forth this, which ye now see and hear. For David is
not ascended into the heavens: but he saith himself,
The Lord said unto my Lord, Sit thou on my right
hand, Until I make thy foes thy footstool.

Also read the bad experience of Stephen in Acts 7:55–58.

But he, being full of the Holy Ghost, looked up
steadfastly into Heaven, and saw the Glory of God,
and Jesus standing on the right hand of God. And
said, behold, I see the heavens opened, and the
Son of man standing on the right hand of God.
Then they cried out with a loud voice, and stopped
their ears, and ran upon him with one accord, and
cast him out of the City, and stone him: and the
witnesses laid down their clothes at a young man's
feet, whose name was Saul.

The evidence is clear that our Lord and Savior came and
completed all his heavenly Father's assignments and went back to
heaven from whence he came to be with his heavenly Father at his
right hand on the throne.

The apostle Paul asked a question one day, trying to avoid
confusion on the various beliefs being displayed all about the city.
Paul was conscious of the divisions of people going in multiple

directions when everyone should have been on one accord in Christ. And even now in our present time, there are still divisions in the body of Christ. The apostle Paul's question is recorded in 1 Corinthians 1:12–13, "Now this I say, that every one of you saith, I am of Paul; and I of Apollos; and I of Cephas; and I of Christ. Is Christ divided? Was Paul crucified for you? or were ye baptized in the name of Paul?" The apostle Paul was generating the understanding that all the followers of Christ should be on one accord.

Jesus wants all his followers to be on one accord, with sisterly and brotherly love that will identify us as his sheep. What he does not want is for us to put him before his Father and worship him as though the Father is old, retired, and out of the mainstream. Jesus is the door to the heavenly kingdom and the one that volunteered to come and redeem us, and so our Lord and Savior, Jesus Christ, the Son of the Almighty God, is to be called upon at any time we need to because there is power in the name of Jesus.

Our heavenly Father has put enormous power in Jesus's hand. We just need to always remember that there is no confusion in the Trinity as we see this various confusion among the brethren in churches. Jesus will be the one coming back at the Father's appointed time to separate the sheep from the goat in the various churches because there are a lot of wolves in sheep clothing and a lot of goats among the sheepfold.

Jesus encourages us in many instances to first recognize the Father. In Matthew 5:16, it reads, "Let your light so shine before men, that they may see your good works, and glorify your Father which is in heaven." Jesus did not say, "They might glorify me, Jesus."

Jesus desires for all our praises and glory to be directed to our heavenly Father, which will go through him as the cushion between the almighty God and us because he is not jealous of that as the other enemy of God does. Jesus truly wants us to understand that everything we see, feel, eat, drink, and enjoy comes from the Father through him. He wants us to recognize the heavenly Father as our provider and the one we should pray to for everything in his name. Matthew 7:7–11 reads,

> Ask, and it shall be given you: seek, and ye shall find; knock, and it shall be opened unto you: For every one that asketh receiveth; and he that seeketh findeth, and to him that knocketh it shall be opened. Or what man is there of you, whom if his Son ask bread, will he give him a stone? Or if he ask a fish, will he give him a serpent? If ye then, being evil, know how to give good gifts unto your children, how much more shall your Father which is in Heaven give good things to them that ask him?

Jesus did not say for us to ask him. Jesus wants to always put the Father first in all things because the Father is first in all things. Jesus does not want us to get it twisted in our thinking and action. Matthew 10:19–20 reads, "But when they deliver you up, take no thought how or what ye shall speak: for it shall be given you in that same hour what ye shall speak. For it is not ye that speak, but the Spirit of your Father which speaketh in you."

Our loving Lord and Savior Jesus is willing to share his divine Father in heaven with all who believe and are willing to follow him to his Father's kingdom. He wants us to understand that even the Holy Spirit, which is the working force of God, is directed and given to help us in everything by his Father and our Father, who is in heaven. Sisters and brothers, young and older soldiers in the army of the Lord, please adjust your thinking so you will always remember that Jesus does not want us to put him first before the Father.

Jesus, Jesus, Jesus, oh, what a wonderful name, the Lily of the Valley, Bright as a Morning Star, the Rose of Sharon. He loved us so much that he was happy to take on the sins of the whole world and carry the cross forty and two miles from Pilate's home to Calvary for all humans. Jesus did all of these good deeds because he loved and obeyed his heavenly Father. Jesus could have spoken and given angels command to squash the actions of all the soldiers that had come to get him, but instead he humbled himself before his heavenly Father because it was not the Father's will in removing the cup that Jesus was about to partake of for the benefit of mankind.

Therefore, brothers and sisters, we have to always adore and praise the name of Jesus. Since he went back to heaven to be by his Father side, observe the powers he had left behind when he came to walk on this earth besides the great ocean. Preaching and teaching the good news of his Father's kingdom were all put back into his hands because his heavenly Father loved him as he loved his heavenly Father.

Jesus just wants us to understand that all the powers he has at his disposal are given to him by his heavenly Father, and so he desires for us to glorify the Father more than himself. Again we go to the Bible, our God-given book of sustenance. In Matthew 11:25–30, Jesus gave all of us, those he spoke to that day, and everyone else who would come for as long as the world lasts a clear and concise understanding that we should open our hearts and minds and allow the Holy Spirit to help us digest this spiritual nourishment.

> At that time Jesus answered and said, I thank thee, O Father, Lord of Heaven and Earth, because thou hast hid these things from the wise and prudent, and hast revealed them unto babes. Even so Father: for so it seemed good in thy sight. All things are delivered unto me of my Father: and no man knoweth the Son, but the Father; neither knoweth any man the Father, save the Son, and he to whomsoever the Son will reveal him. Come unto me, all ye that labour and are heavy laden, and I will give you rest. Take my yoke upon you, and learn of me; for I am meek and lowly in heart: and ye shall find rest unto your souls. For my yoke is easy, and my burden is light.

Our Father and Supreme God, I pray that you will bless this reading of your words in the name of your Son, Christ Jesus. This invitation from God, the Son of the almighty God, should be embraced by every human walking on the face of this earth.

But because of the eating of the fruit of the Tree of Knowledge of Good and Evil and this dreadful evil and the sins it shared is still rampant on the earth, not everyone that the good seed is sown upon their heart will believe and bear spiritual fruit. Because of sin, so many human hearts are like the stony ground that, no matter how pricked their heart gets when they hear the Word of God, it will not last long in their feelings and allow changes in their lives. But we, the children of God the Father, are not in any position to give up on anyone, and so we will continue to tell the good news of God's kingdom until the Lord comes. It is not over until it is over.

Jesus desires that we truly take the time to learn who he really is, and to do that, we have to get into the words of God that have been given to us so freely and allow the Holy Spirit to connect with our inner spirit and teach us because only the Holy Spirit knows the things of God. When he connects with our spirit, a revelation of significant magnitude will come upon us that we will say, "Wow!"

Connecting with the Holy Spirit is what is missing in the lives of many Christians, which is causing them to function as if they are going in the wrong direction, causing them not to be able to stop from doing things that are harmful to the temple of God. Jesus said, "If a person honestly and sincerely takes his yoke, they shall find rest for their souls." We live in a restless world, people struggle to find peace for their troubled souls, and many are looking in the wrong places for peace of mind.

The righteousness of those who truly find it will shine forth as the sun in the kingdom of their Father, and Matthew 13:43 says, "Who hath ears to hear let him hear." People are more concerned about material things and the concerns of man than the things of God. That is why Jesus had to speak harshly to his up-front apostle Peter to give us all the understanding that the things of God the

Father are not a joke or to be toyed with in disrespect. Let us visit what happened between Jesus and Peter in Matthew 16:21–27.

> From that time forth began Jesus to show unto his disciples, how that he must go unto Jerusalem, and suffer many things of the elders and chief priests and scribes, and be killed, and be raised again the third day. Then Peter took him, and began to rebuke, saying, Be it far from thee, Lord: this shall not be unto thee. But he turned, and said unto Peter, Get thee behind me, satan: thou art an offence unto me: for thou savourest not the things that be of God, but those that be of men.

> Then said Jesus unto his disciples, If any man will come after me, let him deny himself, and take up the cross, and follow me. For whosoever will save his life shall lose it: and whosoever will lose his life for my sake shall find it. For what is a man profited, if he shall gain the whole world, and lose his own soul? or what shall a man give in exchange for his soul? For the Son of man shall come in the glory of his Father with his angels; and then he shall reward every man according to his works.

My sisters and brothers in Christ, young and older, let us not just be concerned about the blessings from God in material things that so many people think that material things proved without a doubt that God loves them. All these things we can see before us are temporary. No U-Haul truck and nice, big car haulers are traveling behind any hearse to the graveyard. So getting as many material things as the heart desires and is not connected with Jesus is vanity because none of what is achievable here on earth can buy anyone an apartment in heaven. The heavenly host is seeing all the works of humans here on this planet. Whether they are good or bad, that is done. Many people are losing their souls for riches.

The laws of men are at the forefront more than the laws of God. Every word that Jesus spoke has power in them because he had power as he walked among men. We need to consider deeply what Jesus said in Matthew 24:14–33. In my spirit, because I am writing to born-again Christians, I feel that these verses of the scripture should be brought forth in my writing because of their seriousness and urgency.

And this gospel of the Kingdom shall be preached in all the world for a witness unto all nations; and then shall the end come. When ye therefore shall see the abomination of desolation, spoken of by Daniel the prophet, stand in the holy place, (whoso readeth, let him understand:) Then let them which be in Judaea flee into the mountain: Let him which is on the house top not come down to take any thing out of his house: Neither let him which is in the field return back to take his clothes. And woe unto them that are with child, and to them that give suck in those days! But pray ye that your flight be not in the winter, neither on the sabbath day:

For then shall be great tribulation, such as was not since the beginning of the world to this time, no, nor ever shall be. And except those days should be shortened, there should no flesh be saved: but for the elect's sake those days shall be shortened. Then if any man shall say unto you, Lo, here is the Christ, or there; believe it not. For there shall arise false Christ, and false prophets, and shall show great signs and wonders; insomuch that, if it were possible, they shall deceive the very elect. Behold,

41

I have told you before. Wherefore if they shall say unto you, behold, he is in the desert; go not forth: behold, he is in the secret chambers; believe it not.

For as the lightning cometh out of the east, and shineth even unto the west; so shall also the coming of the Son of man be. For wheresoever the carcase is, there will the eagles be gathered together. Immediately after the tribulation of those days shall the sun be darkened, and the moon shall not give her light, and the stars shall fall from heaven, and the powers of the heavens shall be shaken:

And then shall appear the sign of the Son of man in the heaven: and then shall all the tribes of the earth mourn, and they shall see the Son of man coming in the clouds of heaven with power and great glory. And he shall send his angels with a great sound of a trumpet, and they shall gather together his elect from the four winds, from one end of heaven to the other. Now learn a parable of the fig tree; When his branch is yet tender, and putteth forth leaves, ye know that summer is nigh: So likewise ye, when ye shall see all these things, know that it is near, even at the doors.

Verily I say unto you, This generation shall not pass, till all these things be fulfilled. Heaven and Earth shall pass away, but my words shall not pass away. But of that day and hour knoweth no man, no, not the angelss of heaven, but my Father only. But as the days of Noe were, so shall also the coming of the Son of man be. For as in the days that were before the flood they were eating and drinking,

> marrying and giving in marriage, until the day that
> Noe entered into the ark, And knew not until the
> flood came, and took them all away; so shall also
> the coming of the Son of man be.

How long will this sinful world continue with all the evil and destruction of all kinds? No one knows but the father in Heaven. I have written the words of Jesus and let those that believe continue to get their houses in order, and those that do not believe will be like all those outside Noah's ark after the door was closed and could not be open to anyone cries. As Christians, we cannot believe some of the words of Jesus. We have to believe everything that he spoke to his disciples that is transcending generations until he comes again.

So we are warned by the Son of God himself, and blessed will be those that take heed and continue doing what is right in the eyes of our heavenly Father. It is not even in our interest to speculate on God's timing. It could be tomorrow, next week, next year, or even ten or fifty years from now. No one knows. We just need to acquire the mindset of the five wise virgins who trimmed their lamps to get the extra needed lamp oil and waited for the master.

Jesus said, like in the days of Noah, people were doing their thing as usual, marrying, which takes lots of planning. And of course, lots of construction was going on, and many long-term planning, I am sure, was occurring in the books. But all the time, the man of God kept on preaching that something terrible was going to happen. And to so many then, his message was sounding too strange for their comprehension. Rain! They probably said this guy needs to stop eating those mangoes and that other stuff he cooked that we smell coming from his kitchen.

Now as Christians and followers of the Son of God, Jesus, we know Jesus is coming back, and so something is going to happen as he said it will. As we try with the help of the Holy Spirit to keep our own houses and affairs in order, we are also telling as many as we can to come to Jesus. There are churches on just about every corner in some cities, yet so many people pass by them as if they are not visible. We will continue to sow the words of God as seeds and pray that some will grow with the help of the Holy Spirit.

God's enemy, Satan, knows that his time is running out, and he has ramped up his cunning attack, trying to acquire as many souls as he can to go down with him. Beware, everyone. There is a prowling spiritual lion out there with a lot of helpers that we call demons, going about seeing who they can have for supper and crossing them off in his book. We as Christians know that the enemy is here to steal, kill, and destroy. Please, my brothers and sisters, young and older, tighten your armor from top to bottom to be able to withstand. Let the world come to God even by our actions of Christian living and the love we show among ourselves. Oh, what a day that will be when the Father tells the Son in heaven that the time is now.

There is going to be a lot of weeping and gnashing of teeth. Jesus said to hope it is not in winter when it is freezing everywhere. It is like 9/11. Everybody was doing their usual thing, going to work or at work. Some night shift people were sleeping. Children in school were making noise while their teachers were trying to educate them. Others were deceiving somebody in more ways than one, and the usual noise at Wall Street concentrated on the market trading. Then with everyone but the evil ones unaware, the destructions began that will leave a sad story for generations to come.

Jesus said again in Matthew 24:42–44,

> Watch therefore: for ye know not what hour your Lord doth come. But know this, that if the goodman of the house had known in what the thief would come, he would not have suffered his house to be broken up. Therefore be ye also ready: for in such an hour as ye think not the Son of man cometh.

I, the author of this book, have been called by our heavenly Father through the appointment of the Holy Spirit to preach and teach the good news of God's kingdom and the return of the Son of God for over fifty years.

And so I have no desire to sit and write to make the world laugh. My heart is set steadfast on the things of God to inspire, educate, encourage, and generate determination in the body of Christ so the children of God can be strong in these troublesome times. There is more than enough negative news in the world as it is. I am glad that my help is not needed over there. My calling is to work in the body of Christ, so I have no time for plots and schemes or made-up trickery scenes. "Jesus is coming back sooner than many think" is my message to all who will read and receive it.

Our heavenly Father has been doing, is doing, and will continue to do what the will of the almighty God is to do. We humans have to regularly check ourselves before we wreck the boat that is carrying us over these rough waters of life. Now is not the time to be playing church. Jesus is patiently waiting at the right hand of his heavenly Father for the command to finish the promise that he gave to all his followers, that he has gone to prepare a place and that he will come again and receive all the sheep-minded people to go back with him to his heavenly Father's kingdom.

Immediately after, he separates them from the many goats that are everywhere, among them having a form of godliness but not sincere in their hearts. Even pastors are sitting on many pulpits in three-piece suits, telling the people only what they want to hear and watering down the Word of God to fit in their schemes. And the first ladies wear their wide-rimmed hats to impress the other ladies. And who unto you wolves in sheep clothing, you will be uncovered when you think it is time to be comfortable.

Jesus, the Lamb of God that will break every chain to give us the victory over sin, is ready whenever his Father gives him the go sign. John, the blessed one that was among us here on earth, told us what he saw in the time of his revelation. Let's reflect on the vision of John. Revelation 5:1–10 reads,

And I saw in the right hand of him that sat on the throne a book written within and on the backside, sealed with seven seals. And I saw a strong angel proclaiming with a loud voice, Who is worthy to open the book, and to loose the seals thereof? And no man in heaven, nor in Earth, neither under the Earth, was able to open the book, neither to look thereon.

And I wept much, because no man was found worthy to open and to read the book. neither to look thereon. And one of the elders saith unto me, weep not: behold, the Lion of the tribe of Judah, the root of David, hath prevailed to open the book and to loose the seven seals thereof. And I beheld, and, lo, in the midst of the throne and of the four beasts, and in the midst of the elders, stood a Lamb as it had been slain, having seven horns and seven eyes, which are the seven Spirits of God sent forth into all the Earth. And he came and took the book out of the right hand of him that sat upon the throne.

And when he had taken the book, the four beast and the four and twenty elders fell down before the Lamb, having every one of them harps, and golden vials full of odours, which are the prayers of saints. And they sung a new song, saying, though art worthy to take the book, and to open the seals thereof: for thou wast slain, and hast redeemed us to God by the blood out of every kindred, and tongue, and people, and nation; And hast made us unto our God kings and priests: and we shall reign on the Earth.

Because of the obedience of Jesus carrying out the Father's wishes, we have been redeemed by his sacrificial blood on the cross. Now we all can speak directly to the Father through Christ Jesus, our Lord and Savior, the one worthy to open the book of his Father. Thank you, heavenly Father, for being who you are and demonstrating to us how much you love your human creation.

Thank you for allowing your Son Jesus to come and save us from the bondage of sin. Thank you, Father, for your Holy Spirit that you allow Jesus to dispatch to help us in all things along our new life journey, and thank you for the working of your angels in helping to guide and protect us here on earth as we walk through the valley and shadow of death on this planet each day. Amen.

4

God's Love Is the Substance That Holds the Universe Together

Because the Holy Spirit of God inspires this book, it is of much spiritual sustenance for both the author and everyone else that God will bless those who read it. As I am inspired to dig deep into the awesomeness of God's love, which is too much to grasp without much pondering, I am motivated to start with us as Christians. Jesus told us on many occasions about the love between himself and his heavenly Father. He spoke that this church he personally built upon a solid rock that the wind and the rain of any storm or not even the open gate of hell will be able to tear it down is a product of love.

This church of love is not comprised of mortar, steel, and brick, but human hearts, individual people who will assemble themselves together to praise and worship the Father in heaven. Within this gathering of born-again sisters and brothers, a certain type of character must be displayed that will allow the unbelievers to know that we, the people of God, are different and walking in the path of Christ. In showing and demonstrating that the same love between him and his Father also exists between us, it should be worldwide among all followers of Jesus Christ.

Love is a precious commodity that cannot be bought in a superstore or from any person. So many people get disappointed and suffer great sadness because they think they could purchase someone they love and receive the same love in return. Love is born in the heart of humans as it is in the heart of God. All of God's creations are created with and out of love and are operated with love that will never die. That is why the Planet Earth keeps orbiting around the sun all these millions of years.

When the Bible says that God is love, his love is the glue that binds all creation together. Before we expand the love of God as it holds all things in the universe together, brothers and sisters, as new born-again children of God, we must understand the love of God and its far-reaching action and take the time to ponder this and many other scriptures that edify us to allow love to be born and grow in all of us. For our benefit, please let us take the time to read 1 John 4:1–21 and apply the teaching of apostle John in our lives, as he also was inspired to teach us to love.

BELOVED, BELIEVE not every spirit but try the spirits whether they are of God: because many false prophets are gone out into the world. Hereby know ye the Spirit of God: Every spirit that confesseth that Jesus Christ is come in the flesh is of God: And every spirit that confesseth not that Jesus Christ is come in the flesh is not of God: and this is that spirit of antichrist, whereof ye have heard that it should come; and even now already is it in the world.

Ye are of God, little children, and have overcome them: because greater is he that is in you than he that is in the world. They are of the world: therefore speak they of the world, and the world heareth them. We are of God: he that knoweth God heareth us; he that is not of God heareth not us. Hereby know we the spirit of truth, and the spirit of error. Beloved, let us love one another: for Love is of God; and every one that loveth is born of God, and knoweth God. He that loveth not knoweth not God; for God is Love.

In this was manifested the Love of God toward us, because that God sent his only begotten Son into the world, that we might live through him. Herein is Love, not that we loved God, but that he loved us, and sent his Son to be the propitiation for our sins. Beloved, if God so loved us, we ought also to love one another. No man hath seen God at any time. If we love one another, God dwelleth in us, and His Love is perfected in us. Hereby know we that we dwell in him, and he in us, because he hath given us of his Spirit. And we have seen and do testify that the Father sent the Son to be the saviour of the world.

Whosoever shall confess that Jesus is the Son of God, God dwelleth in him, and he in God. And we have known and believed the Love that God hath to us, God is Love; and he that dwelleth in Love dwelleth in God, and God in him. Herein is our Love made perfect, that we may have boldness in the day of judgment: because as he is, so are we in this world. There is no fear in Love; but perfect love casteth out fear: because fear hath torment. He that feareth is not made perfect in Love. We

love him, because he first loved us. If a man say,
I love God, and hateth his brother, he is a liar: for
he that loveth not his brother whom he hath seen,
how can he love God whom he hath not seen? And
this commandment have we from him, that he who
loveth God love his brother also.

The Bible made it plain as the daylight, no prancing around
the bushes. If a genuine person with the love of God is among any
congregation and it is known that the love of God is not operating
freely in and among everyone and cannot be easily fixed, then that
person is in the wrong crowd. No one is authorized to water down
the words of God to suit their agenda, no one. The word *love* is
enormous, and so it is separated into seven individual segments for
our understanding of love and how to direct this unique nature of
God that is within us from God. Within the Christian church that
Christ Jesus founded upon the solid rock, agape love is considered to
be the number-one and highest form of love originating from God
through Christ Jesus for all humans worldwide.

The agape love is a very selfless kind of love that is given from
the heart, where true love is generated. It is given freely without the
expectation of receiving anything in return. This agape love is sown
in us by God, and if allowed to grow to its full potential, there is
nothing in this world that will be able to take it out of the heart, and
it will be distributed in any way, condition, or circumstance. Even
when someone hurts you very badly, the agape love within you will
still allow you to pray for them.

The agape love cannot dwell among hatred in the heart. This
love will help you survive difficult times and situations, even in
families where everybody cannot seem to get along. It will also
help you to work hard in your place of worship to generate a good
atmosphere where love can be sown. And with the help of the Holy
Spirit, it will begin to grow that it will be witnessed that sisters and

brothers are communicating with each other and helping each other as it should be in the name of Jesus.

Agape love is the umbrella under which all the other love should operate. Storge love is the kind of love that some parents have for their children, and it is regrettable that not every parent possesses this love. That is one of the many reasons we witness so many single parents. Storge love is also between brothers and sisters and other family members through the fondness of familiarity.

The love that many people get happiness and sadness from is eros love. Eros love in the Christian community is encouraged to come alive in marriage. It is a passionate and romantic love that is evident in the desire to be in the company of another and is displayed through physical affections in holding hands under the night stars, kissing, or hugging. This love has been abused and brought sadness to many because many people only desired another person's physical body or even just the glitter, glamour, or what is referred to as bling, nice cars, money, and other material things. Satan has used and is still using this eros love feeling to destroy many with fornication and adultery, of which Christians are overly warned against. This physical love attraction will keep anyone from entering the kingdom of God, and on the flip side, when it is grown in the right soil of marriage, it is beautiful. Christians, the Bible said, it is better to marry than to burn or fall in sin. When two people are married, eros love can allow them to grow old together with smiles on their faces.

The principle of God's love is why the planets, including Earth, revolve around the sun. And other found planets orbit their stars as the Earth does the sun. God is all love, humans learned to love, and so many humans born on this planet live, grow old, and die and never learn how to love. For us humans, the word *love* is used for good and evil because someone will say "I love you" and truly mean it from their heart. Then others will say "I love you" with deception in their heart. So many people have been disappointed in hearing the word *love* and it never producing fruits for them. When

Christians say "I love you," it should and must be genuine from the heart because we flow with God's agape love.

This chapter will examine some practical functions that operate in such an orderly manner that it is impossible not to discern the characteristics of love in their operation. I believe that God's love is in all creation. In my opinion, the vast technological world that we now are a part of and enjoying, even in the use of electrical power, that we cannot envision doing without. Think of the so many other electronic devices that we can't leave home, all because of the attraction principles of the source of love that exists in the atom, the foundation and the source of the electrical functioning.

The atom is what everything incorporates. There are different numbers of atoms in various substances. The electricity we use every day is an excellent place to start in my concept of demonstrating God's love circulating in and around creation. To understand the theory of how electric current flows, you must understand something about matter and what it is made of. The matter is made up of atoms, the smallest amounts of a substance that can exist.

Atoms are made up of protons, neutrons, and electrons. The number of electrons in an atom is the same as the number of protons. Protons and neutrons are located at the center, or nucleus, of the atom. Protons have a positive charge. Neutrons have no charge. Electrons have a negative charge and orbit around the nucleus, in a manner very similar to the way the planets orbit around the sun. Electrons move around the nucleus in different spaces or shells, which are at different distances from the nucleus of the atoms.

For example, a copper atom has twenty-nine protons and twenty-nine electrons. A hydrogen atom has only one proton and one electron, and they look like this in their operation.

Drawing
When sufficient energy or force is applied to an atom, the outer electrons become free and can move around the proton, hoping to

get to it because of the love attraction that exists between them. Once this knowledge was made clear to the scientist, the electrical evolution began. And that is the birth of electricity, or the origination of the precious power that lights up the cities at night, allowing us to watch television, helping us to see our way to the bathroom at night, and facilitating our navigation process on our smartphone to help us in our travel so we turn right or left as it instructs us more than once to make sure we do not mess up and go in circles.

There is the possibility of learning something new in my explanation of electricity for those who are not aware or familiar with its movements to do the job it is forced to do. I am able to share this knowledge of electricity because I am a trained electronic technician and electrician and from the same source of agape love, which is the topic of this chapter. I consider this knowledge that our loving heavenly Father has allowed me to acquire a blessing, and I am delighted that I can help someone with such interesting and unique information. To God be the glory for all the marvelous things he has blessed humans to enjoy on this earth.

Please enjoy as we go forward. Here are two different elements, the protons and the electrons in the atom, like a man and a woman. The proton is positive in its nature; the electrons are negative in its nature. The proton sits still in the center of the atom, while the electron, when allowed, keeps circling, trying to find a way to connect with it out of what I am describing as a love attraction. If given the opportunity, or a path, this electron will do everything possible to get to this proton. Once this yearning attraction was discovered, intelligent humans decided then to help this electron find its way while it helped us along its journey in getting to its destination.

So let's think of a battery that everyone is familiar with. The battery has two terminals. One is called the positive, which represents the proton, and the other terminal is called the negative, which represents the electron. If someone would connect a piece of wire at the positive terminal and then touch the negative terminal, it would create a huge spark.

Because of the lust and excitement of the negative electron getting its wish to rush to the love it is longing to be with and if both ends stayed connected, the battery would be destroyed very quickly. This rush of electrons getting to the proton without any interruption is what is called a short in a circuit, which causes a fuse to blow, wires to burn, breakers to trip, and equipment to burn up in other electrical operations.

This overzealousness and excitement of these electrons have to be controlled or slowed down. It is like a young man encountering a beautiful young lady and falling head over heels in love with her and developing a problem sleeping at night. He even begins to lose his appetite as his mother discerns that he was not eating as much as he used to.

Out of her curiosity, she inquires of her son and gathers the understanding that this young lady's beauty has got a hold on her son, and so the mother has to try to slow him down a little by telling him, "Son, you have to take your time to know her. My son, I can see that you want so much to be with this young lady, but you have to slow down."

This urgent love attraction also happens to young and older ladies because as long as we live, love for the opposite person will always exist. The controlling way to deal with the love rush of these electrons in electricity is to put them to work, which is what causes the lights to shine so brightly for all of us to enjoy the family gathering at home at night or see our way better driving in the city at night. Wherever there is light, the moods or feelings will always elevate. How beautiful it is to see the sunrise in the mornings and give the daylight until it is time to move along as it seems, but we know the Earth is doing the movement around the sun.

Here is how we will slow down these lovers of electrons. Think of the wire connected to the battery. Instead of the electrons rushing straight to the other side, we will put a light bulb in its way. The light bulb is made up of a small, special kind of wire called the filament, and this filament presents a resistance to the flow of these electrons. For instance, when the electrons travel, say from the negative side of the battery, it encounters this filament resistance on the way to getting to its love, the proton, on the positive side of the battery.

It will not turn back because it is eager to get to where it desires to be, so it pushes and tussles with this filament resistance until the filament gets hot, and bam, there is light for us. The electrons continue at a slower, controlled pace and make contact, with both of us being happy with the light and the electron in finally reaching its destination.

When you are driving or being driven, consider the lovely music from the radio being played, the lights to see where you are going, and the horn you can blow, like they used to do a lot in New York City when another car in front of you is slowing you down or stopping in your way. All these operations exist because the electron from the negative side of the battery is trying to get to the positive side. It is being forced to do this work on its way to the desired destination.

So now, it is revealed that wherever and whenever the lights are on in the house, the park, the hotel, or the city streets, the knowledge is shared that these lights are caused by the negative electrons fighting their way through these resistance filaments to get what I describe as the love they are longing to be with. Maybe there is a name for this kind of love, as we do have many other names for the various functions of love. And the beats go on.

In all electrical and electronic equipment, the same principle of traveling electrons allows humans to live large and prosperous, as if we are imitating the good life in the garden of Eden. To God be the glory for all he has done and is allowing humans to do, and so the big question is, "Why is every human on this planet not praising and giving our loving heavenly Father the honor, praise, and worship he so much deserves?"

There is also another beautiful love attraction of one element to another, which is called magnets. Magnets are used in just about every industrial operating plant, robots, and many other functions. Many people have the knowledge of the attraction of magnets and just may not look at it in this way of the universal love that exists in creation. There are natural magnets from nature, and there are man-made magnets called electromagnets.

A magnet is described as having two different poles on the two ends of a rectangular magnet or on the opposite side if it is round. One end is called the north pole; the other end is called the south pole. When a north and south pole are facing each other, an attraction begins, and the closer they get to each other, the stronger the attraction becomes. If they are allowed to touch each other, they will embrace each other and will not want to let go of each other.

When the two south poles are facing each other, they repel, or push against each other, so it is said of magnets that unlike poles attract and like poles repel. God is love, and so everything in creation is a product of his love and therefore incorporates his love in various forms. Although the Earth orbits the sun and is designed not to touch it, I believe the same principle of love attraction keeps it orbiting for millions of years.

The awesomeness of God cannot be easily spoken with words because he is too great for humans to comprehend the totality of his greatness and powers. Humans have only been discovering new galaxies and other planets and gathering the knowledge and understanding of even our own Planet Earth in minimal numbers of years.

The huge space telescope and other eyes in the skies are constantly looking and searching to understand some of the mighty precious accomplishments of God. Technology is all in and around in nature. When God had finished with his creation, he said that everything was good, so God does not need to keep tweaking things, unlike man's creations.

The more thankful we are to our heavenly Father, the better life we can live because we cannot exist outside of the umbrella coverage of his love and favor. It is mind-boggling when anyone has the opportunity to be exposed to the study of electronics and the various components in technology and how they operate as individuals, with each one doing what it is assigned to do in such an order of humility with no complaint.

God creates all things and blessed humans to acquire the knowledge to use his creation to prolong our existence. I would like to share another technology understanding with my readers. Thank you very much for taking the time to enjoy this wonderful and edifying information concerning the awesomeness of our loving heavenly Father and his vast creation.

God's love for us should be echoed in every place on this planet when we consider all the wonderful living conditions made possible by the wisdom, knowledge, and understanding that he had blessed humans to acquire. When Jesus was here on earth, he often used earthly things to describe heavenly functions and even himself when he spoke about the one corn being put in the ground and how many more corns would be reaped.

Jesus could have used other technology words, like cell phone, television, internet, cable box, and Twitter, since he was aware of the future and the things we are enjoying now, but the people then would not have the slightest idea of what he was talking about and probably would be thinking of how strange he had become. So to God be the glory for the fact that I can use the word *television* to explain another incredible way that the awesome knowledge of God is working for our good on this earth.

Please remember the first explanation of how everything electrical and electronics work because of the love attraction of the negative electrons pushing their way through every and anything that will allow them to travel through it to get to the positive protons.

There are two types of traveling electrons voltage that do outstanding work for all of us. One voltage is called alternating current (AC). The other voltage is called direct current (DC). The AC voltage is constantly moving. Please imagine or, if you can, draw a straight line as I will explain this movement. It starts at the left side of the line going upward about an inch, which we will call the positive peak. Then in a forward direction, it comes back down, this time passing the line to the same one-inch distance, which we call the negative peak.

Then still in a forward direction, it goes back up and stops at the line. This is called one AC electrical cycle. In the United States, the AC voltage repeats this cycle sixty times per second, too fast for the human eyes to follow it. For instance, when you are looking at the light in the house, it is going on and off sixty times per second, too fast for your eyes to tell the difference, so it seems to stay on all the time.

The DC voltage flows as just a straight line, meaning it is a continuous voltage. As I mentioned, the word *television* can be used in our time, and everyone knows what I am talking about, unlike when our Lord and Savior was conducting his earthly ministries. If you do not know, please keep learning a little about the inner first stage of the voltage going in for the television to show you the football game.

This television is plugged into the electric wall socket. In this socket, there is only the AC, or alternating voltage, the one that moves or changes a lot. The television, however, needs the DC, or direct current, voltage to operate. This is the voltage that looks like a straight line.

You are wondering how this happens, and I will gladly share this knowledge with you. Earlier in our reading, I mentioned that many electrical components or individual parts work together in electronic technology. To get our television going, we need a couple of different parts to supply the correct voltage. We will use a transformer to step the voltage down to the proper amount.

That is what a transformer is made to do. It has two different sets of wires wrapped in circles but not touching each other. Let's imagine the wrap to the left has a hundred wraps, or turns, and it is called the primary side of the transformer. The wrap, or turns to the right, has only twenty wraps or turns, and we call it the secondary side of the transformer. We can also refer to this transformer as a step-down transformer because the primary side has more turns than the secondary side.

When the television is plugged into the wall socket, the AC voltage goes to the primary side of the transformer because the two wraps of wires become two magnets but do not touch each other; the primary magnet induces a voltage into the secondary wire or magnet. The amount of voltage it induces is based on how many wraps the secondary side has.

For example, the wall outlet is standard with 120 volts of electricity in the homes, but the television only needs 18 volts to operate. Inside the television, various components use a different amount of voltage to work. We are just looking at what is called the power supply that gives voltage to all the other parts or components.

Because of the help of the transformer, we have the lower voltage, but it is still AC that is changing rapidly, and we need DC voltage that stays constant. Here we have Mr. Diode, a component or part that only allows the AC voltage to go one way, up, but not down or forward but not backward. The diode is an example of how someone would be born again or become changed from what they used to be. It changes how the voltage was operating into something else. The diode is called a converter because of how it converts or changes the voltage.

Once the AC voltage goes through the diode, it is no longer AC. It is closer to becoming DC or will be going straighter than before. What it needs now is someone to give it a hand in getting rid of what is called ripples. And so there is a filtering circuit, which uses another component called a capacitor that does filtering to straighten it out, and after the filtering, we have DC, or the straight voltage from the power supply, that goes in a different direction to supply the many television circuits with the various voltage that they need.

We can say then that the television is connected to the secondary side of the transformer and the electricity coming in from the wall socket is connected to the primary side of the transformer. Our God is so awesome in how he created humans with the ability to learn different things in life, which is why we have so many professions that help people with one thing or another.

A fragment or a piece of God's love is in everything in this universe: animals, insects, flying creatures, plants, trees, grass, and even the galaxies and planets as they orbit, staying in their own lane. Some have more love in them than others, like God's special creation, humans. Some people have more love in them than others.

There is so much knowledge in technology to learn, and our loving heavenly Father is the master and the originator of all technology. I did not even scratch the surface of information contained in the operation of television. I just quickly touched base about the initial power supply. I would encourage a study in some form of technology to anyone.

It is truly unique. So many awesome wonders are performed in medical, science, communication, and robotic technology because of the love of God. There is nothing that exists throughout creation that God is unaware of or does not carry God's love elements and fragments.

Everything in the creation of God shares in a fragment of his extraordinary intelligence and his merciful love. And they all praise God in one way or another: the sun, the moon, the stars, the birds, the animals, the fish in the sea, the flowers, trees, grass, and the insects.

The beautiful and technological achievements that humans can accomplish are only a testimony of a small fragment of the wisdom of God. God is worthy to be praised and be glorified by all of his creation. All that I want to do for the rest of my life is amplify the praises and thanksgiving that our heavenly Father deserves.

The heavenly host has never left us or forsaken us, and they will never change the love and blessing that they have already pledged to humanity. Each of us should always put forth the effort required to enjoy our lives to the fullest in righteousness, giving thanks every day for God's favor and blessings upon us. Share in divine agape love to all that we can in helping, giving, and above all praying for all the leaders of the world and everyone else, especially those that are so less unfortunate.

5

Heaven Helps Us All

To all my Christian sisters and brothers worldwide, I pray the ultimate blessings from heaven upon each one of you right now, in the majestical name of Jesus, even as you read this chapter. To our heavenly Father be all the praise, honor, and glory forever and ever. And not only do I pray for my brothers and sisters in Jesus Christ, because as Christians, we are mindful not to pray in a selfish manner, so I am also praying for all the people of the world who are not Christian, of every other religion, nation, culture, and language. Amen.

"Heaven helps us all," cries out from the hearts of so many people around the world who are dealing with and experiencing so many different kinds of situations, hardships, and loss of loved ones. Some do not know where their next meal will be coming from or do not have a permanent roof over their heads. Many are trying to escape from their own countries in fear of losing their lives and the lives of their family, along with so many other kinds of life troubles that people are facing. I would kindly and lovingly introduce the teaching of the most famous prayer at this time as our Lord and Savior taught us how to pray, which is called the Lord's Prayer.

In Matthew 6:1–13, Jesus gave a knowledgeable understanding of what our mindset and heart condition should be when communicating with our heavenly Father.

> TAKE HEED that ye do not your alms before men, to be seen of them: otherwise ye have no reward of your Father which is in Heaven. Therefore when thou doest thine alms, do not sound a trumpet before thee, as the hypocrites do in the synagogues and in the streets, that they may have glory of men. Verily I say unto you; they have their reward.
>
> But when thou doest alms, let not thy left hand know what the right doeth: That thy alms may be in secret: and thy Father which seeth in secret himself shall reward thee openly. And when thou prayest, thou shall not be as the hypocrites are: for they love to pray standing in the synagogues and in the corners of the streets, that they may be seen of men. Verily I say unto you, They have their reward. But thou, when thou prayest, enter into thy closet, and when thou hast shut the door, pray to thy Father which is in secret; and thy Father which seeth in secret shall reward thee openly."
>
> But when ye pray, use not vain repetitions, as the heathen do: for they think that they shall be heard for their much speaking. Be not ye therefore like unto them: for your, Father knoweth what things ye have need of, before ye ask him. After this manner

therefore pray ye: Our Father which art in Heaven, Hallowed be thy name. Thy Kingdom come. Thy will be done in Earth, as it is in Heaven. Give us this day our daily bread. And forgive us our debts, as we forgive our debtors. And lead us not into temptation, but deliver us from evil: For thine is the Kingdom, and the power, and the Glory, for ever. Amen.

All praises are to our heavenly Father for sending his Son, Christ Jesus, who personally knows the Father and heaven and taught us the right way to think about the tremendous wisdom of our heavenly Father that knows everything we need even before we ask of him. Before we begin to ask our loving God to supply our needs, we want to be sure that we honor him and give him the highest praise that we humans possible can in words by saying "Hallelujah" to his most Holy Name. We can also be sure to honor our God in our daily living and what we do in the ministry of the kingdom. Many churches and Christians do not often refer to God's name recorded in Psalm 83:18, but I feel it necessary to quote it here for all my readers. "That men may know that thou, whose name is JEHOVAH, are the most high over all the earth."

In the beginning, God created heaven and earth and all that is in them. It is clear to everyone understanding that heaven was created before the earth, although no one really knows the time between the two creations. It could have been a million or thousands of years. We believe that heaven is a place where no flesh and blood exist, and so it contains only super-intelligent spiritual beings that feel no pain like humans do and the throne of God, the Supreme Creator.

Heaven is a place of peace, love, community, and worship, where God is surrounded by a heavenly court and all his working angels. Jesus, the Son of God who came from heaven to earth to show us the way, taught us to pray to the Father that his kingdom would come here on earth as it is in heaven.

It is taught that there are three levels of heaven: the celestial, terrestrial, and telestial kingdoms. It is also understood that the first heaven is actually the atmosphere that contains the things we can see, such as clouds, birds, and airplanes. Whenever we fly in an airplane, we are flying in the first heaven. According to scientists, the first heaven extends about twenty miles above the earth.

It's amazingly comforting that Jesus mentions heaven in 192 verses in the New Testament. No humans have ever been and will never be able to go to heaven in the flesh. However, John, the Revelation writer, is caught up in the Spirit on the isle of Patmos. He was very blessed to be so much filled with the spiritual power that his spirit, and not his flesh, was invited to take a spiritual journey, as we read in Revelation 4:1–11.

> AFTER THIS I looked, and, behold, a door was opened in Heaven: and the first voice which I heard was as it were a trumpet talking with me; which said, come up hither, and I will show thee things which must be hereafter. And immediately I was in the Spirit: and, behold, a throne was set in Heaven, and one sat on the throne. And he that sat was to look upon like a jasper and a sardine stone: and there was a rainbow round about the throne, in sight like unto an emerald. And round about the throne were four and twenty seats: and upon the seats I saw four and twenty elders sitting, clothed in whiter raiment; and they had on their heads crowns of gold.

> And out of the throne proceeded lightnings and thunderings and voices: and there were seven lamps of fire burning before the throne, which are the seven Spirits of God. And before the throne, there was a sea of glass like unto crystal: and in the midst

of the throne, and round about the throne, were four beasts full of eyes before and behind. And the first beast was like a lion, and the second beast like a calf, and the third beast had a face as a man, and the fourth beast was like a flying eagle. And the fourth beasts had each of them six wings about him; and they were full of eyes within: and they rest not day and night, saying, Holy, holy, holy, Lord God Almighty, which was and is, and is to come.

And when those beasts give glory and honour and thanks to him that sat on the throne, who liveth for ever and ever, The four and twenty elders fall down before him that sat on the throne, and worship him that liveth for ever and ever, and cast their crowns before the throne, saying, Thou art worthy, O Lord, to receive glory and honour and power: for thou hast created all things, and for thy pleasure they are and were created.

To God be the glory for seeing John worthy of writing the book of Revelation. No other humans have ever gotten a glimpse of the things John heard and saw in the Spirit realm. The king thought that he was putting John away, but lo and behold, he was helping John get to the place where God needed him to be away from the noise and combustion of people and things so the heavenly host could truly communicate with him. The Holy Spirit of God can use us for the kingdom work wherever we are. Often when a man says no, God will say yes. Let us keep our focus on the things of God. Satan will always use people and earthly things to try to distract us, but with the help of the Holy Spirit, we will prevail.

Heaven will help us all—Yes!—from that moment in time when God said, "Let us make man in our image, after our likeness: and let them have dominion over the fish of the sea, and over the fowl of the air, and over the cattle, and over all the Earth, and over every creeping thing that creepeth upon the Earth. So God created man in his own image, in the image of God created he him; male and female created he them."

Genesis 1:26–27 reads, "And our loving Heavenly Father, even after these blessed humans disobeyed his command and enter into sin by being subdued by the cunning serpent that was under the control and influence of satan." Genesis 3:7 says, "And the eyes of them bothe were opened, and they knew that they were naked; and they sewed fig leaves together, and made themselves aprons." Look at the action of our merciful God in verse 21, "Unto Adam also and to his wife did the Lord God make coats of skins, and clothed them."

Ever since that moment in time, so long ago through centuries and generations, our loving God has never stopped helping his humans creations. So keep looking up to the heavenly hill where all our help comes from because all our help comes from God, the Creator of heaven and earth. Hallelujah to his Holy Name. Jesus showed to people gathered to see and hear him the power of provision that had existed even in him here on earth one day. The apostle John reflected on the event in John 6:1–14.

> AFTER THESE things Jesus went over the sea of Galilee, which is the sea of Tiberias. And a great multitude followed him because they saw his miracles which he did on them that were diseased. And Jesus went up into a mountain, and there he sat with his disciples. And the passover, a feast of the Jews, was nigh. When Jesus then lifted up his eyes and saw a great company come unto him, he saith unto Philip, Whence shall we buy bread, that these may eat? And this he said to prove him: for he himself knew what he would do.

Philip answered him, Two hundred pennyworth of bread is not sufficient for them, that every one of them may take a little. One of his disciples, Andrew, Simon Peter's brother, saith unto him, There is a lad here, which hath five barley loaves, and two small fishes: but what are they among so many? And Jesus said, Make the men sit down. Now there was much grass in the place. So the men sat down, in number about five thousand.

And Jesus took the loaves; and when he had given thanks, he distributed to the disciples, and the disciples to them that were set down; and likewise of the fishes as much as they would. When they were filled, he said unto his disciples, Gather up the fragments that remain, that nothing be lost. Therefore they gathered them together, and filled twelve baskets with the fragments of the five barley loaves, which remain and above unto them that had eaten.

Heaven is the only place where all humans can rely on in confidence and trust that God will hear our prayers in the name of Jesus. As Christians, we look to heaven from whence came the Holy Spirit as we give God the praise, honor, and glory. There are no places on this planet where the sun does not shine or the day and night do not appear. And the blue sky is out of view unless, of course, you are underground. JEHOVAH-JIREH (God will provide), our loving heavenly Father, allows the rain to fall on everyone. Our loving heavenly Father allows the sun to take over and bring daylight after the dark night presents itself for everyone. Our loving heavenly Father will provide for everyone in one way or another.

King David testified to this same known fact in Psalm 23.

THE LORD is my shepherd; I shall not want. He maketh me to lie down in green pastures: he leadeth me beside the still waters. He restoreth my soul: he leadeth me in the paths of righteousness for his name's sake. Yea, though I walk through the valley of the shadow of death, I will fear no evil: for thou art with me; thy rod and thy staff they comfort me. Thou preparest a table before me in the presence of mine enemies: thou anointest my head with oil; my cup runneth over. Surely goodness and mercy shall follow me all the days of my life: and I will dwell in the house of the Lord for ever.

This psalm of David has been embraced worldwide by people of all nations. Our loving heavenly Father cares for every one of his earthly children, of which I am one. David's inspiration to pen this psalm took him way down deep inside of himself and had him reflect maybe back to when he was a little shepherd boy. The more he pondered how God had protected and provided for him, the more passionate he became in the writing of Psalm 23. As a young man looking after the sheep day after day, the inspiration of the Holy Spirit reminded him of how passionate and caring he was and how many times he could have lost his own life-fighting animals to protect his sheep. David knows the characteristic of a good shepherd.

That is why he could have said from deep within his heart that the Lord is my shepherd. People worldwide join David in this same sentiment. Just to reflect on the fact that our mother could have gotten an abortion or had a miscarriage, our heavenly Father made sure that we came into this world when we took our first breath of life outside of our mother's womb.

Think of the life experience God allows us to have and are still having, how he protected us from seen and unseen danger, how he did not allow Satan's weapons that were formed against us to prosper, and how he made a way out of no way for us. God helped some of us to make it when we did not think we would be able to go on. He put food on our table and a roof over our heads. Let's stop for a minute because I think it's time for us to say, "Thank you, heavenly Father. Hallelujah to your most Holy Name forever and ever. You are God."

And then God's loving Son, Christ Jesus, volunteered to come from his Father's side in heaven to earth to show us the way and voluntarily allow the working of Satan to put him up on the cross to pay for all our sins. When Satan, the rulers, and the crowd that day thought they were doing wrong to him, they were doing what he had come to the earth to have them do. They just did not know the extent of the good they were doing that day when in their mind, they were doing him wrong, putting him up on the cross between the two thieves with a big sign over his head saying, "This is Jesus, the King of the Jews," mocking him, and wagging their heads as they passed by and said, "If thou be the Son of God, come down from the cross." People worldwide know, not just believe, that he could have come down from that cross if he had chosen to do so, and people worldwide are very happy that Jesus did not.

Jesus, as the word that the apostle John said, was with God before he came to earth. He is back in heaven at his Father's side again, still making petitions for us and waiting on his Father's command to return and receive the church he has built upon a rock that is still standing tall. Oh, when I think of the goodness of Jesus and all he has done for me, my soul cries, "Hallelujah! Thank God for saving me."

Then after Jesus returned to heaven, the Holy Spirit agreed to leave his holy place to come here to earth, which was evident on the day of Pentecost, to oversee and be the administrator of the church and to depart various gifts to humble and willing soldiers in the army of the Lord so the kingdom message can be spread throughout the whole world before Jesus's return.

Over and over again, God has shown his deep, unwavering love to us. Jesus has demonstrated his love for us in more ways than one. The Holy Spirit is here with us and has shown his love for us humans day and night. All this love that is shown and the beautiful things that have been done for humans—not from New York, San Francisco, or Paris, but from a place far from the reach or sight of humans—is definitely not on this planet but from heaven. Can heaven help us all? I will allow each reader to answer this question within their own heart. In my heart, I know that the heavenly host will always be helping us until Jesus gets permission from the Father to do what he is waiting to do. Hallelujah.

So as children of God, and as I am a living witness of God's grace, mercy, and goodness, I will continually encourage everyone and anyone to keep trusting God, who might not come within the twenty-four hours we are accustomed to because God is not limited to our 24/7 time system. A day to our heavenly Father is like a thousand years, although he knows when and how to address each of his earthly children's concerns and problems.

God always proceeds by the power of his Holy Spirit at the right time for all of us worldwide. However, in view of the many marvelous things that heaven is doing for us, God has also given us the power within ourselves to choose right from wrong. Jesus, who helps to create us, knows we are capable of doing and following guidelines, and he encourages us to do the things that are righteous before his heavenly Father.

That is why, in Matthew 5:1–16, Jesus has provided an abundance of spiritual nourishment that we need to feast on and allow every bit of what he says to sink deep down into our good heart soil so it can bear spiritual fruits for the world to see and come to the knowledge of God.

> AND SEEING the multitudes, he went up into a mountain: and when he was set, his disciples came unto him: And he opened his mouth, and taught them, saying, Blessed are the poor in Spirit: for theirs is the Kingdom of Heaven. Blessed are they

that mourn: for they shall be comforted. Blessed are the meek: for they shall inheret the Earth. Blessed are they which do hunger and thirst after righteousness: for they shall be filled.

Blessed are the merciful: for they shall obtain mercy. Blessed are the pure in heart: for they shall see God. Blessed are the peacemakers for they shall be called the children of God. Blessed are they which are persecuted for righteousness' sake: for theirs is the Kingdom of Heaven. Blessed are ye, when men shall revile you, and persecute you, and shall say all manner of evil against you falsely, for my sake.

Rejoice, and be exceeding glad: for great is your reward in Heaven: for so persecuted they the prophets which were before you. Ye are the salt of the Earth: but if the salt have lost his savour, wherewith shall it be salted? it is thenceforth good for nothing, but to be cast out, and to be trodden under foot of men. Ye are the light of the world. A city that is set on an hill cannot be hid.

Neither do men light a candle, and put it under a bushel, but on a candle stick; and it giveth light unto all that are in the house. Let your light so shine before men, that they may see your good works, and glorify your Father which is in Heaven.

Heaven, please help us all. For all the things Jesus mentions, if they are done in the right way, blessings will be achieved.

Jesus knows he was speaking with both those disciples then, and people throughout the generations until now possess the God-given abilities to function very well in each of those tasks because he was there that day when we were being created. And he knows all the characteristics that were placed in us to do good works on this earth.

God knows everything about each of us individually, and no one needs to repeat what Jonah did, trying to hide from God. King David helps us all to understand that the more humble we are before the almighty God, the better things will go for us. We cannot use psychology on God. Who knows what we will think before we even think it? Psalm 139:1–18 reads,

> O LORD, thou hast searched me, and know me. Thou knowest my down-sitting and mine uprising, thou understandest my thought afar off. Thou compassest my path and my lying down, and art acquainted with all my ways.
>
> For there is a word in my tongue, but, lo, O Lord, thou knowest it altogether. Thou hast beset me behind and before, and laid thine hand upon me. Such knowledge is too wonderful for me; it is high, I cannot attain unto it. Whither shall I go from thy Spirit? or whither shall I flee from thy presence? If I ascend up in Heaven, thou art there: if I make my bed in hell, behold, thou art there. If I take the wings of the morning, and dwell in the uttermost parts of the sea; Even there shall thy hand lead me, and thy right hand shall hold me.
>
> If I say, surely the darkness shall cover me; even the night shall be light about me. Yea, the darkness hideth not from thee; but the night shineth as the day: the darkness and the light are both alike to thee. For thou hast possessed my reins: thou hast covered me in my mother womb. I will praise thee; for I am fearfully and wonderfully made: marvellous

are thy works; and that my soul knoweth right well. My substance was not hid from thee, when I was made in secret, and curiously wrought in the lowest parts of the Earth.

Thine eyes did see my substance, yet being unperfect; and in thy book all my members were written, which in continuance were fashioned, when as yet there was none of them. How precious also are thy thoughts unto me, O God! how great is the sum of them! If I should count them, they are more in number than the sand: when I awake, I am still with thee.

God knows where each one of us is in our lives. Heaven has always been helping all of us in one way or another and will continue to be there for us because our loving heavenly Father does not change and his love for the human creation will never run out of caring.

Giving God the glory, praise, and honor should be a daily routine for all of us that are breathing the breath of life. In 2020, Earth's population was counted to be 7.753 billion people, and now, here in 2021, the number has risen to 7.9 billion people. As huge as the number is to us, God knows each one individually. It is not like in some overcrowded church where many members are just numbers, too much for the pastor to shake hands, and some do not even try to greet the faithful.

There are 195 countries today worldwide, and the Spirit and presence of God and the heavenly host can see everyone how awesome and majestic our God is. "Hallelujah" to his most Holy Name. The design's unique reproduction process is one of the super blessings that our awesome God had worked out in planning to make the first man and the first woman.

Sometimes because of the hustling and bustling of the way the world turns, we do not take the time to ponder or meditate on the marvelous, delicate, and unique creative process of our supreme God. He is allowing humans to have children that, generation after generation, could continue to go on and on even to us in our generation and will continue into the future until God says otherwise.

Genesis 1:27–28 reads,

> So God created man in his own image, in the image of God created he him; male and female created he them. A God blessed them, and God said unto them, be fruitful, and multiply, and replenish the earth, and subdue it: and have dominion over the fish of the sea, and over the fowl of the air, and over every living thing that moveth upon the earth.

So God had already planned and put the reproduction process in place long before he had a conversation with them, and that was the beginning of the family because they eventually had two sons in time.

So God himself, along with Jesus and the heavenly host, creates the family atmosphere. God then loved the idea of father, mother, and children in their home long before Adam and Eve had children, and he knows generations of people would come. I think God also wishes for the family to stay together or marriages to be taken very seriously, but because of sin and the breakdown of human's closeness to God, people do not stay together as long as some think that they would. I have pondered why some couples stay together for forty, fifty, sixty, and seventy years and others have various times before separation.

Heaven's blessings are upon everyone and every family worldwide. The breakdown of families, in my opinion and not a scientific study, is frequently because of sin and selfishness in one or more people. In reality, some things in life are meant to be, and others are not. There are many reasons why some relationships do not last as long as they were hoped for. Motives, reasons, faith, love, and lust are why relationships get started. Let's look quickly at these, and of course, they might not be the only ones. Motive is a one-sided functioning and is often about why one person wants to achieve a certain goal without sincere consideration of the other person's feelings.

Reason is why someone develops feelings for another. Is the reason based on things that can easily be faded away, like money, bling-bling, a nice car, house, or a good job? Unfortunately a layoff happens, and the excellent job is no more. And so goes that up-front feeling as well. Faith is someone whose mind was on accomplishing a specific goal or being a faithful Christian and was not really seeking a partner, but through what we would be called faith works, they were in the company of another. By chance, the chemistry, or spiritual working, they both get swept off their feet.

Does anyone believe in love at first sight? Many people do. The first time that eyes were laid on them, I felt it in my bones that this was the one, and it also happens that sometimes both people can feel the same thing simultaneously. True love does exist. I think this is the love that lasts the longest because it seems that these two people love each other for themselves for who they are, and getting to know each other was very easy, like everything just falls into place and gets stronger and stronger over time as if it were meant to be that way.

I think most people's love grows after the initial excitement if it were properly cared for, and both parties love being together and respecting each other and were willing to work the kinks out as they go and grow together. Love does grow like a delicate plant that has to be cared for with plenty of loving spiritual nourishment. Since God himself is the one that had ordained the first marriage, the most blessed marriage relationship, in my opinion, is the one that is rooted in the words of God and is under the umbrella of many prayers.

It would often seem that the fleshly (lust) takes center stage in today's sin-filled world. Lust is just wanting to mesh with another person, trying to parade itself as love, like wolves in sheep's clothing. It is speaking many nice words with lyrics like a nice love song, and if the listeners are not careful, they can be overcome with the thought that maybe this is the one. On this side of love is the most heartbreak and sadness. Many single mothers came from this type of affection. Not everyone is following the words of God, and they are suffering hardship because they allow Satan's influences to overtake them.

In my over fifty years of ministry, I have witnessed many marriages that lasted for a very long time. I will mention one couple, using their names as I have permission from them, Alvin and Joyce Howard. They have been married for forty-five years, and I inquired about them because they are godly, devoted Christians and was told that they have always believed that people who pray together stay together. They said that no relationship is perfect because we are all living in an imperfect world, but the love they have for each helped them over many steep mountains they have encountered. They said the Holy Spirit was there to help calm stirring vibes, and they learned to compromise out of respect for each other.

May heaven continue to bless and help us all in and through our various situations as we all travel down the troublesome roads of life. I will always continue to encourage anyone and everyone that I believe are without the dependency on the Most High God and his blessings on our lives.

With the help of the Holy Spirit through the blood of our loving Savior and Redeemer, Christ Jesus, there will always be vexation of spirit that will generate all kinds of breaking down of the flesh that will lead to sickness. Do what is right before the heavenly host, resist the many temptations and lustful desires of the flesh, be faithful in your relationship, and never forget the words of the Bible that Satan is going about like a roaring lion, always seeking out who he can devour.

6

Heaven-Bound: Righteousness Recipe

To God be the glory for everything he has done for every human born on Planet Earth. God created us in his own image and likeness, and everyone has their individual testimony of God's love and goodness. People worldwide have different experiences in their lives, but whatever it was, good or not-so-good, God brought you through, and you are still here to be reading these pages, so to God be the honor, praise, and glory to his most Holy Name that he so much deserves. John 3:16 reads, "For God so loved the world, that he gave his only begotten Son, that whosoever believeth in him should not perish, but have everlasting life."

Suppose you are a Christian, meaning that you are a born-again, committed follower of Jesus Christ. In that case, you most likely are familiar with the comforting words of our loving Savior, Jesus, the Son of God. John 3:1–3 reads,

> Let not your heart be troubled: ye believe in God,
> believe also in me. In my Father's house are many
> mansions: if it were not so, I would have told you. I
> go to prepare a place for you. And if I go and prepare
> a place for you, I will come again, and receive you
> unto myself; that where I am, there ye may be also.

There in that Bible reading, we began putting together the recipe with the word *belief.* Jesus is saying to us that if we really and truly believe in God as we should as becoming a Christian, then we should not have any issues in believing in him also since he is the Son of God. If we sincerely believe in him, we should not have any problem believing what he says about his knowledge of his heavenly Father's many mansions.

We believed that Jesus rose from the tomb in which they had placed him on the third day, just like he said because when they went to inquire about him that Sunday morning, they were astonished to see that the stone was rolled away and he was not inside. Can you comprehend the amazement, the look on their faces they had, Mary, who was first, and especially Mr. Simon Peter? Yes, that same bold Simon who wanted to draw his sword to defend Jesus and still denied him three times because of fear of losing his life in all that skirmish that was taking place.

Don't laugh at Peter because even now, after so many years have gone by, many Christians are still nervous and shy about proclaiming Jesus in various places. Each one of us knows where we stand in that conversation. Moving along to the righteousness recipe, the main reason that all or most people became followers of Christ is the promise of everlasting life.

And so we have the determination of keeping the heaven-bound focus as our main and most significant goal in our life. Propel us now in these troublesome and perilous times that we are living. Be very knowledgeable that reaching our goal requires that we button up our armour of God very tightly, since we are not fighting or wrestling against flesh and blood, but against principalities, unseen spiritual powers, the ruler of the darkness of this world, and spiritual wickedness in high places.

The spiritual recipe requires us to make it into heaven when we transition from the fleshly pain-filled body into a new spiritual body that does not associate itself with any kind of pain. This heaven-bound righteousness recipe is more than salt, pepper, onion powder, kicking chicken seasoning, garlic powder, and all the other nice seasonings used to produce a nice-tasting meal. On the day of our baptism, we received the diploma to practice righteousness in starting our new life with the Lord. And so from that day onward and for the rest of our days on this side of the grass, we are new, born-again children of God. And the life we live will tell on us.

In this chapter, nothing new is really being created. I am just bringing the word of God to remembrance as an inspiration, motivation, and spiritual encouragement to Christians worldwide and everyone else who might read these lines and want to give their lives to Christ. Because no matter how long anyone has been a Christian, the newborn soul still receives the same promise of life everlasting with Jesus. The ingredient of our spiritual recipe could start with a lot of different scriptures, but let us begin with the heartfelt pledge that we will cultivate and grow the fruit of the Spirit: love, joy, peace, long-suffering, gentleness, goodness, faith, meekness, temperance, and temperance.

As born-again Christians, we have to allow the Holy Spirit to guide us as we walk with him. We have to walk in and again with the Spirit daily because there are many other lifestyle conducts that we cannot afford to mix into our recipe for the kingdom. We have to always remember that God's enemy, Satan, will always be setting a net for Christians in the form of temptation, but with us walking with the Holy Spirit, we are confident that no weapon that he tries to form against us will bear fruits, but of course, as we also know, he will never stop, so we have to be quick to recognize his cunning tactics and be ready to rebuke him in the name of Jesus.

Some of the things we definitely do not want in our spiritual recipe that will help us to God's kingdom is adultery, fornication, uncleanness, lasciviousness, idolatry, witchcraft, hatred, variance, emulations, wrath, strife, seditions, heresies, envyings, murder, drunkenness, and revellings. In the mighty name of Christ Jesus and with the power of the Holy Spirit, I pray right now for myself and everyone else who will have the opportunity to read these pages that our loving God and heavenly Father will not allow any temptation to overthrow us and cause us to mix these actions in our spiritual recipe that keeps us heaven-bound.

As Christians and soldiers in the army of the Lord, Christ Jesus, let us stand with our loins girded about with truth, making sure we have on the breastplate of righteousness and, of course, our feet shod with the preparation of the gospel of peace. Hello, soldiers! Let us not forget to take the shield of faith because the darts of the wicked one is fiery, and while we are at it, let us not forget to take and put on the helmet of salvation. When we get the nod from the Holy Spirit that will connect with our inner spirit, we will step out with the Word of God, our spiritual sword. Sisters and brothers in Christ, this is not a joke from across the pond. Spiritual warfare is very real, strong, and getting worse day by day.

The heaven-bound spiritual recipe could also include, for longevity, the encouragement of another brother from long ago, who was also under the influence of the Holy Spirit and wrote for us this righteousness life-living nourishment when he said, with my interpretation also,

> Blessed is the man [man, woman, young, and older] that walketh not in the counsel of the ungodly. [We should not join in with unbelievers or people that we know are not of God in their plans to do wrong and evil deeds.] Nor standeth in the way of sinners. [We have to be careful where we hang out or the company we keep as Christians.] Nor sitteth

in the seat of the scornful. [If someone is feeling or expressing contempt or ridicule, with a feeling of attitude or expression of contempt looking down on someone else, being scornful, mocking, and making fun of someone else, if you cannot help that person do better, do not sit with them and become a part of it.]

But his delight is in the law of the Lord [There are blessings from God, and any person would find it pleasurable to do what is right before God], and in his law doth he meditate day and night. [Waking up in the morning with a godly song in your heart and even throughout the day, you can't help but ponder and think how good it feels doing what is right before God. It is because God's favor and blessings are filling your spiritual cup.] And he shall be like like a tree planted by the rivers of waters. [You will feel very grounded and spiritually strong when your conscience is clear and you are maintaining clean hands and are pure your heart.]

That bringeth forth his fruit in his season. [Good fruits will come within time; your labor will not be in vain, but do good because what is sowed the same will be reaped.] His leaf also shall not wither. [When you are grounded in God and doing what is right, everything that is connected to you like the leaf to the tree will be blessed.] And whatsoever he doeth shall prosper. [When the favor and blessings of God are on us, whatever we do will have his blessings, and who God blesses, no man can curse.] The ungodly are not so. [Being ungodly is the opposite of being godly, and they do not inherit the same blessings from God.]

But are like the chaff which the wind driveth away. [When a person is not grounded in God, it is like the man that built his house on the sand and got blown away in the storm.] Therefore the ungodly shall not stand in the judgment. [Jesus will separate the sheep from the goat so, after the separation, the goats won't be a part of the conclusion.] Nor sinners in the congregation of the righteous. [After the separation, no more ungodly goats will be among Christ's sheep to influence or corrupt them.]

For the Lord knoweth the way of the righteous. [People can fool other people sometimes but cannot fool God at no time. God knows our hearts and thoughts, so we should check ourselves before we wreck ourselves.] But the way of the ungodly shall perish. [Having an ungodly heart and living an ungodly life is like being on a sinking ship where Satan is the captain and everyone is going down and will perish.]

The heaven-bound righteous living recipe combines godly spiritual fruits blended together and taken one every day like a one-a-day vitamin. Many tout a scripture every day that will keep the devil away. Perilous times are upon us; there is no time to be straddling the fence of good and evil. Step out from evil into the law of God. If you have not already done that, please ask Jesus to come into your heart. The Holy Spirit will step in and put you on the right road leading to God's kingdom. John 8:51 reads, "Jesus said, 'Verily, verily, I say unto you, if a man keep my saying, he shall never see death.'"

Please always pray that our loving heavenly Father will allow his Holy Spirit to help and keep us as we walk through the valley of the shadow of death. But always remember that death is for the ungodly only. When it is time for one of Jesus's sheep to come home to him, a transition takes place faster than the blinking of your eye, from the fleshly body to a spiritual body.

Like the five wise virgins that prepared themselves and were ready when their master came, be ready by living each hour of each day as if it might be your last hour or day on this planet. No one will ever know when the master and your day will come. For the born-again believer, living and walking in righteousness, an angel will be by your side to prepare you for the transition. As natural as we know this fleshly life to be, so is the spiritual life also, where the ones who transit with clean hands and remain pure in their heart will see God the Father, God the Son, and God the Holy Spirit, all the heavenly host.

Flesh and blood cannot enter the kingdom of God. So as long as we are in the flesh, we have to feast on the righteous living recipe, which are the righteous laws of God that he has blessed and allowed to be assembled together in one place and is called the Holy Bible. Everyone is encouraged to get more into reading God's words and not only read them but ask the Holy Spirit to help, teach, and allow us to apply the laws of God in our daily lives. Please be mindful of the word (daily). Just Sunday worship alone will not be enough to safeguard us from the terrible snares of the enemy of God.

As we first help ourselves, let us help others get to where we are as we strive to move forward to higher ground. Let us be careful not to be judgmental and look down on anyone because where they are, we also were. Let's reflect now on some counseling of wisdom in a letter from the apostle Paul to a church where Titus was the one in charge, whom Paul described as his own son because of the spiritual oneness between them. He encouraged Titus to counsel the Christians there in all righteousness.

Titus 3:1–7 reads,

> PUT THEM in mind to be subject to principalities and powers, to obey magistrate, to be ready to every good work. To speak evil of no man, to be no brawlers, but gentle, showing all meekness unto all men. For we ourselves also were sometimes foolish, disobedient, deceived, serving divers lusts and pleasure, living in malice and envy, hateful, and hating one another.
>
> But after that the kindness and love of God our Saviour toward man appeared, Not by works of righteousness which we have done, but according to his mercy he saved us, by the washing of regeneration, and renewing of the Holy Ghost; Which he shed on us abundantly through Jesus Christ our Saviour; That being justified by his grace, we should be made heirs according to the hope of eternal life.

Sisters and brothers, young and older, did you see what I saw in that reading of the scripture? In case you missed it, it is the hope of eternal life that got me so excited. Please excuse me. I know everyone reading this chapter is aware of that. Eternal life is living forever, not in this pain-filled body that we are currently in, but in a new, spiritual pain-free body.

We will not be dealing with high blood pressure, diabetes, cancer, heartbrokenness, the hunger that so many are experiencing, and the worrying of not being hit by a stray bullet, as did a wonderful lady who traveled to see her son inducted in a place of high regard. Unfortunately she was sitting in the way of bullets from these unruly guys on the street below her and others sitting enjoying a nice conversation. She was hit and lost her life. How sad.

Everybody, of course, would like to enter in through the pearly gate of heaven, although no one is raising their hands that they are ready. As Christians, we have to live our lives in readiness because no one knows when the transportation angel is going to pull up beside us and we have no choice but to get on board for the cool ride to our permanent home.

Thank you, heavenly Father, that we can dream of being with you one day. Thank you, Jesus, that you have done so much to make it possible for us, and thank you, Holy Spirit, for the guidance, teaching, assistance you are giving us with our righteous living, and spiritual protection from all unseen evil forces.

The heaven-bound spiritual recipe contains an enormous amount of spiritual nourishment that will keep every child of the great Creator filled that there will not be any need to vary off the narrow path that leads to the kingdom of God. Let's ponder this addition to the spiritual recipe in Colossians 3:1–6.

> If ye then be risen with Christ, seek those things which are above, where Christ sitteth on the right hand of God. Set your affection on things above, not on things on the Earth. For ye are dead, and your life is hid with Christ in God. When Christ, who is our Life, shall appear, then shall ye also appear with him in glory.

> Mortify therefore your members which are upon the Earth; fornication, uncleanness, inordinate affection, evil concupiscence, and covetousness, which is idolatry: For which things sake the wrath of God cometh on the children of disobedience. In the which ye also walked some time, when ye lived in them. But now ye also put off all these; anger,

> wrath, malice, blasphemy, filthy communication
> out of your mouth. Lie not one to another, seeing
> that ye have put off the old man with his deeds;
> And have put on the new man, which is renewed in
> knowledge after the image of him that created him:

In every city you might visit, there is a certain street that separates north and south and another that separates east and west. The separating of the old man and then becoming the new man is done on the day of baptism. On that day when we were driving or being driven to get to where the baptism was going to take place, that was the old man in the car. Then we waited patiently through the service and sometimes felt like the preacher was trying to step on somebody's toes, but all he was doing was telling the truth. And then the time finally came to be submerged under the water.

The pastor in place, along with the elders or deacon in the pool, waited for the old man to step in, which we did. The old man listened for the pastor to finish, and then at the end, after confirming with us that we understood what we were doing and what we were about to do was being done by our free will, he said, "In the name of the Father, in the name of the Son, and in the name of the Holy Spirit." And there you went, being held with strong arms to raise us back from under the water, and when they did, we arose and stood up before the congregation a newborn spiritual person. From that day, it can be said that we are born-again.

Water baptism symbolizes our dedication to the heavenly Trinity: the Father, the Son, and the Holy Spirit. This dedication should be from the heart in all sincerity and conviction of our inner spirit. This water baptism concept was also done to Jesus, in which he allowed himself to be an example for the entire world to understand that a rebirth from flesh to Spirit is essential to becoming a spiritual child of the Creator. We have heard of John the Baptist, preaching in the wilderness of Judaea, saying, "Repent ye for the Kingdom of God is at hand." Many people in John's day went out to him from Jerusalem and Judaea and others from around the region, and he baptized them in the confession of their sins.

John the Baptist was a very godly man of great integrity who, under the Holy Ghost's inspiration, was as honest as he possibly be to the people who came to him. John did not want to be seen as anything but a servant of God with no pride or ego, craving for any attention to come to him as many preachers are doing now in our time.

In Matthew 3:11, John said, "I indeed baptize you with water unto repentance: but he that cometh after me is mightier than I, whose shoes I am not worthy to bear: he shall baptize you with the Holy Ghost, and fire: Whose fan is in his hand, and he will thoroughly purge his floor, and gather his wheat into the garner; but he will burn up the chaff with unquenchable fire."

Verse 13 continues,

> Then cometh Jesus from Galilee to Jordan unto John, to be baptized of him. But John forbad him, saying, I have need to be baptized of thee, and comest thou to me? And Jesus answering said unto him, suffer it to be so now: for thus it becometh us to fulfil all righteousness. Then he suffered him. And Jesus, when he was baptized, went up straightway out of the water: and, lo, the heavens were opened unto him, and he saw the Spirit of God descending like a dove, and lighting upon him: And lo a voice from Heaven, saying, This is my beloved Son, in whom I am well pleased.

Please reflect on the point of Jesus saying "suffered it to be so now: for thus it becometh us to fulfill all righteousness." Sisters and brothers, baptism is not a game and should be considered a blessing to be able to dedicate ourselves to the kingdom of the great and almighty Creator. Jesus laid out so many examples for us because of his love and his wanting to take as many as he can into his Father's many mansions. Because of our Creator's love for his human creation, we have inherited the best blessing we could ever hope for, for our God so loved the world that he sent his only begotten Son. We are heaven-bound through his Son Jesus.

We still have our human part of continuing righteousness and letting our heavenly Father be proud of us as he was for his servant, Job. Because of Jesus, we are in a better position than where Job was; however, the same Satan showed up in that heavenly meeting and tried to trash Job, who was only faithful because of material things. Let us all learn from Job's experiences because the same Satan is still here among us with his bands of demons creating havoc in the world.

Everything we accumulate is temporary as long as we are on Planet Earth. Someone said they have never seen a U-Haul truck loaded with anyone's earthly achievement riding behind the lifeless body to the cemetery. Enjoy God's blessings in your life to the fullest; we just have to be careful and know that Satan will use the things we love to distract us from our heavenly goal.

To God be the glory forever, in the name of Jesus. We need to maintain a joyful spirit knowing who we are and whose we are. If Christians who are born again and living righteously with a clear conscience, clean hands, and purity in our hearts are always sad, then how can we save souls when we are the ones who have left our troubles at the altar in the hands of the great almighty God? If we cannot retain and maintain a peaceful spirit and countenance, how can we encourage others? The people of God are the ones who have to stand strong and allow our lives to be a living testimony to the world of God's goodness. And like the five wise virgins, be ready for our loving Savior, Christ Jesus.

Jesus leads the way to everlasting life in his Father's kingdom. We only need to follow him. The Bible is our spiritual source of nourishment, full of the righteous recipe to help us on our journey. Helping as many people as we can in the wonderful knowledge of God is a good concept for us to adhere to as we maintain our balance amid the time and seasons with the help of the Holy Spirit. Remember, all Christians are living testimony of God's love to humanity. Therefore, we all should be demonstrating this agape love daily to save others before the coming judgment day when the trumpet will sound as it is written, so it will also be.

I believe that every born-again Christian is a minister of the gospel with the help of the Holy Spirit. Being a spiritual child of the king sitting on the heavenly throne allows us to tell somebody about Jesus and all he has done for humanity. Waiting to get a big title of recognition from between the church's four walls before someone can be saved by hearing something from the Christian person is behind schedule.

The Holy Spirit is in everyone that grace and mercy saved through the shed blood of Jesus the Christ. Once we are connected to Jesus, our responsibility is to help others get connected also. Jesus's message to us is the same as he told Simon and Andrew, his brother, casting their net into the sea, and Jesus said unto them, "Come ye after me, and I will make you become fishers of men" (Mark 1:17).

The spoken words of Jesus are food for our souls, and if we truly digest them and live by them, then the heavenly-bound hope will not be just a dream. Listen to what Jesus said in Luke 6:45–49,

> A good man out of the good treasure of his heart bringeth forth that which is good; and an evil man out of the evil treasure of his heart bringeth forth that which is evil: for of the abundance of the heart his mouth speaketh. And why call ye me, Lord, Lord and do not the things which I say? Whosoever cometh to me, and heareth my sayings, and doeth them, I will show you to whom he is like:
>
> He is like a man which built an house, and digged deep, and laid the foundation on a rock: and when the flood arose, the stream beat vehemently upon

that house, and could not shake it: for it was founded upon a rock. But he that heareth, and doeth not, is like a man that without a foundation built an house upon the Earth; against which the stream did beat vehemently, and immediately it fell; and the ruin of that house was great.

When we read the words of Jesus, we need to ponder them very carefully and deeply because the wisdom in them goes over many heads and is blown across many soils but does not sink therein to take root. Blessed is everyone who indeed hears and does the bidding of the Lord.

Jesus died an earthly death so we may have life and have it more abundantly because once our spirit experiences the transition from this fleshly temple to its new spiritual temple, it does not have to do the same again. The inner spirit that God has created within us knows the Holy Spirit of God because the communication of us knowing that we are children of God comes through this channel. Our spirit is waiting and anticipating to be free from this body of pain, heartbroken, and disappointment. He is ready to go even more than our heart back to where he belongs and from whence he came.

The Holy Spirit of God inspires this book; therefore, the Bible is the foundation on which it stands, not just on the excitement that the authors are feeling about the magnificent things of God and the extraordinary love of Jesus or even the author's words. So please let us hear from the apostle Paul, who will enlighten us with more wisdom concerning Christ and the Spirit of God. 1 Corinthians 2:1–13 says,

> And I, brethren, when I came to you, came not with excellency of speech or of wisdom, declaring unto you the testimony of God. For I determined not to know any thing among you, save Jesus Christ, and him crucified."

And I was with you in weakness, and in fear, and in much trembling. And my speech and my preaching was not with enticing words of man's wisdom, but in demonstration of the Spirit and of power: That your faith should not stand in the wisdom of men, but in the power of God. Howbeit we speak wisdom among them that are perfect: yet not the wisdom of this world, nor of the princess of this world, that come to naught: But we speak the wisdom of God in a mystery, even the hidden wisdom, which God ordained before the world unto our glory: Which none of the princess of this world knew; for had they known it, they would not have crucified the Lord of glory.

But as it is written, Eye hath not seen, nor ear heard, neither have entered into the heart of man, the things which God hath prepared for them that love him. But God hath revealed them unto us by his Spirit: for the Spirit searcheth all things, yea, the deep things of God. For what man knoweth the things of a man, save the spirit of man which is in him? Even, so the things of God knoweth no man, but the Spirit of God. Now we have received, not the spirit of the world, but the Spirit which is of God; that we might know the things that are freely given to us of God. Which things also we speak, not in the words which man's wisdom teacheth; but which the Holy Ghost teacheth; comparing spiritual things with spiritual.

7

Make a Joyful Noise Unto the Lord

To God be the glory, for his mercy endures forever. Psalm 100:1–5 reads,

> Make a joyful noise unto the Lord, all ye land. Serve the Lord with gladness: come before his presence with singing. Know ye that the Lord he is God: it is he that hath made us, and not we ourselves; we are his people, and the sheep of his pasture. Enter into his gates with thanksgiving, and into his courts with praise; be thankful unto him, and bless his name. For the Lord is good his mercy is everlasting; and his truth endureth to all generations.

God deserved all our praises forever. For the sake of clarity and the need for all Christians to be on one accord, let us reflect on the name Lord. The name Lord has appeared in the Old Testament about six hundred times and in the New Testament around seven hundred times. In the Old Testament, this name is a rendering of the distinctive personal name of the God of Israel. Exodus 24:1–3 reads,

> AND HE said unto Moses, Come up unto the Lord, thou, and Aaron, Nadab, and Abihu and seventy of the elders of Israel; and worship ye afar off. And Moses alone shall come near the Lord: but they shall not come nigh; neither shall the people go up with him. And Moses came and told the people all the words of the Lord, and all the Judgements: and all the people answered with one voice, and said, All the words which the Lord hath said will we do.

And even in the book of Genesis, the word Lord is used many times. Genesis 2:7–8 reads, "And the Lord God formed man of the dust of the ground, and breathed into his nostrils the breath of life; and man became a living soul. And the Lord God planted a garden eastward in Eden; and there he put the man whom he had formed."

The author only gave the explanation to clarify the understanding that both God the Father in the Old Testament and Jesus, the Son of God, in the New Testament were both referred to as Lord. Lord signifies a person having power and authority over others. Early Christians viewed Jesus as the Lord. The Greek word *Kynos* means God.

So at the time when King David wrote and said, "Make a joyful noise unto the Lord," he was specifically referring to God the Father. I feel that there is not enough noise that we can make to glorify our loving Creator because he has been so good to his human creation. And how can we not serve God the Father in total gladness?

Everybody in churches worldwide should be on one accord in showing the joy on their faces, happiness, excitement, and gladness in worshiping our loving God. I have gotten down from my seat on pulpits, dancing to the praise music playing and the choir singing from their heart, and saw other Christians in the pew acting like their mind is somewhere else, while so many others are up on their feet clapping hands, dancing, and praising the almighty God.

As the psalmist said in our scripture reading, we always have to remember and let it be known, and I also said to be conscious always that the Lord is God and it is he that has made us. And we are the sheep of God's pasture. We just need to act with a sheeplike character so that God, through the awesome and tremendous power of the Holy Spirit, can lead us day by day through these turbulent waves of life like rough waters.

Sisters and brothers, young and older, when we enter through his gate or door of service, let us hurry in with thanksgiving in our hearts and into his courts with praises and more exciting praises because the Lord our God is good and we need to say "Hallelujah" more than once because God's mercy is everlasting and the truth in the word of God endureth to all generations.

I give honor to all the talented and God-fearing, beautiful gospel songwriters and inspirational singers who are allowing a tremendous amount of praises to flow to our loving Creator in their gospel music. Holding our peace while listening to gospel music being played in our car, stopping the car on the way to work, and giving a dance praise on the side of the road to the inspiring praise music being played on the radio is a thought that many, including myself, have resisted. Sometimes it feels so refreshing waking up early in the morning with God's help with a song in our heart, and family might wonder why singing is coming from the bathroom.

God's Holy Spirit gave a wide variety of assignments to different people to perfect the saints and allow praises, honor, and glory to go up to our heavenly Father. Whatever was put in our hearts to do or perform for the kingdom of God, we should do it with so much joy and excitement that our family members start to wonder what has come over us or if we are drinking the wrong coffee. The Holy Spirit gave some apostles, prophets, evangelists, and pastors and teachers the wonderful ability to sing, which has to be amplified to the fullest. If you find that singing allows others to praise God in your heart, I pray that God will always bless your heart in that dedication.

And excuse me, please, the musicians are to be applauded and taken out to dinner. The gift and ability to play music are so excellent, and some musicians in churches will play to put people on their feet. 1 Peter 4:10–11 reads, "As every man hath received the gifts, even so minister the same one to another, as good stewards of the manifold grace of God. If any man speak, let him speak as the oracles of God; if any man minister, let him do as of the ability which God giveth: that God in all things may be glorified through Jesus Christ, to whom be praise and dominion for ever and ever. Amen."

Blessed is everyone who used their gifts and talent to glorify and generate praises to our heavenly Father. Music is a building block of creation. The great ocean has its own rhythm; the trees generate their music. The singing birds sometimes sound like they get excited with their abilities to sing. The rivers, streams, and even the wind and lots of other things of nature seem to raise their voices in their own way, and I believe that the earth sings itself and raises praises to God. The many galaxies, including our own Milky Way galaxy, planets, and stars, all are known to generate their own sounds. And let us not forget under the great ocean, the ocean's life-forms have a lot of sounds, with the dolphin like a movie star.

Psalm 148:1–14 reads,

> PRAISE YE the Lord. Praise ye the Lord from the heavens: praise him in the heights. Praise ye him, all his angels: praise ye him, all his host. Praise ye him, sun and moon: praise him, all ye stars of light. Praise him, ye heavens of heavens, and ye waters that be above the heavens. Let them praise the name of the Lord: for he commanded, and they were created. He hath also stablished them for ever and ever; he hath made a decree which shall not

pass. Praise the Lord from the Earth ye dragons and all deeps:

Fire, and hail; snow, and vapour; stormy wind fulfilling his word: Mountains, and all hills; fruitful trees, and all cedars: Beasts, and cattle; creeping things, and flying fowl: Kings of the Earth, and all people; princes, and all judges of the Earth: Both young men, and maidens; old men, and children: Let them praise the name of the Lord: for his name alone is excellent; his Glory is above the Earth and Heaven. He also exalteth the horn of his people, the praise of all his saints; even of the children of Israel, a people near unto him. Praise ye the Lord.

Let's take a minute to reflect on King David, who was known as a great musician in his time so long ago. His soft music could calm evil spirits and probably brought many lovers together. Let us read a Bible story concerning this David experience. 1 Samuel 16:14–23 reads,

But the spirit of the Lord departed from Saul, and an evil spirit from the Lord troubled him. And Saul's servants said unto him, behold now, an evil spirit from God troubleth thee. Let our Lord now command thy servants, which are before thee, to seek out a man, who is a cunning player on an harp: and it shall come to pass, when the evil spirit from God is upon thee, that he shall play with his hand, and thou shalt be well.

And Saul said unto his servants, provide me now a man that can play well, and bring him to me. Then answered one of the servants, and said, behold, I have seen a son of Jesse the Bethlehemite, that is cunning in playing, and a mighty valiant man, and a man of war, and prudent in matters, and comely person, and the Lord is with him. Wherefore Saul sent messengers unto Jesse, and said, Send me David thy son, which is with the sheep. And Jesse took an ass laden with bread, and a bottle of wine, and a kid, and sent them by David his son unto Saul.

And David came to Saul, and stood before him: and he loved him greatly; and he became his armourbearer. And Saul sent to Jesse, saying, Let David, I pray thee, stand before me; for he hath found favour in my sight. And it came to pass, when the evil spirit from God was upon Saul, that David took an harp, and played with his hand: so Saul was refreshed, and was well, and the evil spirit departed from him.

The wonderful and lovely gospel music is doing the same for Christians worldwide, refreshing our inner spirit even now in our time, where music is everywhere. So blessed are all musicians using their talents to bring glory and praises to our heavenly Father. Thank God for Jesus, who desires that we direct our honor, glory, and praises to his and our Father in heaven. Make a joyful noise unto the Lord, for he is good. If you had noticed, Saul's servants refer to him as Lord with a lowercase "l" because Saul was over them. Uppercase or a capital "L" refers to God.

All Christians worldwide should be encouraged to listen to gospel music as much as they can and thank God for all the many radio stations dedicated to playing gospel music as far as their signals can be transmitted. And if anyone reading these words has a little or a lot of singing in your heart, please get on the choir in the church that you worship and bring as much richness to the praise team as you possibly can. God will bless you tremendously. You might even sound better singing in church than you are in the showers. The greatest joy every human should enjoy in their lives should be to praise the God that created us and his Son, Christ Jesus, for saving us and giving us everlasting life in a new spiritual body.

Psalm 149:1–5 reads,

> PRAISE YE the Lord. sing unto the Lord a new song, and his praise in the congregation of saints. Let Israel rejoice in him that made him: let the children of Zion be joyful in their King. Let them praise his name in the dance: let them sing praises unto him with the timbrel and harp. For the Lord taketh pleasure in his people: he will beautify the meek salvation. Let the saints be joyful in Glory: let them sing aloud upon their beds.

Heavenly Father, please, in the name of Jesus, give your people a revival, a renewing of heart and spirit. Give us all a mind to praise and worship you in all our doings day by day. Rebuke the evil one we pray so his influences will not interrupt the flowing of prayers and praises of your saints. Father God, you loved us so much even when we did not grasp the power of your love. Forgive us, Father, and continue to bless and keep us as the sheep of your pasture. We will always be mindful to give you all the honor, praises, and glory you so much deserve in the mighty name of your Son, Jesus. Amen.

Psalm 146:1–2 reads, "PRAISE YE the Lord. Praise the Lord, O my soul. While I live will I praise the Lord: I will sing praises unto my God while I have any being." Psalm 146:1 says, "PRAISE YE the Lord: for it is good to sing praises unto our God; for it is pleasant; and praise is comely."

I have been in ministry for over fifty years and have seen and heard many musicians play the organs and piano. It seems that I have had a weakness for spiritual nourishment since I was a child, and of course I grew up in a Christian home. Those of my readers who can relate to that know the drill. I was so drawn in my spirit to the things of the Bible. There were times when I felt as if the Bible book of Proverbs and Ecclesiastes and some other scriptures were my Father speaking to me. I grew up loving God. His words have really been a light for my path. God's words in my heart kept me out of trouble and allowed me to never be locked up or been put in jail, for which I always say, "To God be all the glory forever and ever. Amen."

I will recommend the Bible to all young minds growing up. It is a wonderful thing to remember the Creator of this universe in the days of youth. I have always encouraged children to do what is right because God sees and knows everything. And this generation of our loved ones growing up before us now needs a lot of prayers to go up to the Father in heaven for them and us because their minds are much more advanced than when we were their age, and Satan is targeting the young minds. Good deeds will always win over evil deeds, and Jehovah God is still on the throne of heaven (Psalm 83:18).

Let them also listen to lots of praises and explain that God deserved all our recognition from the young and older people. For us older children of God, remember that no matter how old we live to be, we are always God's children. A day to God is like a thousand years, which no man has ever lived. My encouragement is that if you are not sick and can move around, please dance for the Lord. Clap your hands, tap your feet, and let God see that if loving him is wrong, then we don't want to be right. Every chance we get, we should give God the glory and praise him.

I have a keyboard at home that I do need to put more time into playing. I took two semesters of piano in college but never seemed to work with it as much as I should. The best keyboard player is an adult who grew up playing music from childhood. Even many good singers arose from singing in church as a child. Let me talk for a minute about this first lady of a church in which I was an elder and sitting on the pulpit every Sunday in the reach of the first lady playing praise music.

It was a thrill and so delightful and praiseworthy, and people seemed to always get up around the church when she began to play, dancing in praise and glorifying God. I could never sit there when she started playing. She was so good, and the music was so inspirational. Everyone could hear and feel her love for her God coming down through her fingers onto the keyboard.

She told the congregation the story of how when she was a little girl, she prayed and asked God to anoint her finger so she could play the piano she was exposed to, and in her heart and mind, she truly witnessed the evidence that he did anoint her mind and fingers. And when she is playing, she feels the blessing of God using her to bring blessings to others, so she praises God in playing. Brothers and sisters in Christ, the more thanksgiving we feel in our hearts, the more praises will take place. The Holy Spirit will bring back to our memory where God has brought us from, and we just want to express our heartfelt gratitude in whichever way we can praise our heavenly Father in the name of Jesus.

And so I used to get up from my pulpit seat, even when other elders were still sitting, clapping their hands, tapping their feet, and observing, praising God in their individual way. I got down before the altar or on the side and got my praise on in my own way as the Holy Spirit led me. Praise music causes the tiredness that I sometimes would feel because of getting up at three thirty every weekday morning to go to work to disappear. That praise music gets me moving because I love to praise my Creator.

I do not get up from my seat on the pulpit just to demonstrate that I can dance for the Lord. The Holy Spirit generates a certain feeling. It is a feeling of thanksgiving, a feeling of love for God, a feeling that when it gets built up, it is like Jeremiah describing it as the fire caught up in his bones. There is a personal feeling in every child of God that causes some to just run around the church; others dance like they got happy feet, and even the musicians play like the

Holy Spirit is truly in each of them. King David once said, "I was glad when they say unto me, let us go to the house of the Lord." Blessed are every person that finds joy, peace, comfort, serenity, wholesomeness, and a feeling of being closer to God in the house of the Lord. God is worthy to be praised forever.

Making a joyful noise unto the Lord is my encouragement to every human being on this Planet Earth. Our heavenly Father and Creator, through his only begotten Son, Christ Jesus, and the working power of the Holy Spirit, has done everything, making it possible to receive everyone in the kingdom of heaven that will accept Jesus as the Son of God.

Recognize and believe in their heart and soul that Jesus is the door to the heavenly Father and that no one can go to heaven except through him. The Holy Spirit is here with us to comfort us when we need to be comforted, teach us, correct our path of spiritual travel day by day on the narrow road, and serve as the church administrator.

Jesus went back home to heaven, where he came from, and asked the Holy Spirit to go and take his place here on earth to help us, his new family, to make it into his Father's kingdom. Jesus knows that we as humans could not make it on our own, with Satan as a roaring lion always sniffing out the weak linkage with his cunning, mischievous ways and stirring up strife and confusion even among the people of God. He sets his demons in every place that he can among the people of God as wolves among the sheepfold. As we all know, he is not using snakes anymore as he did in the garden of Eden; he uses people against people in every setting that he can.

With the grace, mercy, and favor of our loving heavenly Father and the Lord Jesus on our side, with the power of the Holy Spirit, no weapon that is formed against the people of God, no matter where in this world the sheep of Christ are, will ever be able to stop the praises, glory, and honor from going up to our God who deserved all our praises and more. Our commitment and confidence are rooted in the words of God. Romans 8:31–39 reads,

What shall we then say to these things? If God be for us, who can be against us? He that spared not his own Son, but delivered him up for us all, how shall he not with him also freely give us all things? Who shall lay any thing to the charge of God's elect? It is God that justifieth.

Who is he that condemneth? It is Christ that died, yea rather, that is risen again, who is even at the right hand of God, who also maketh intercession for us. Who shall separate us from the love of Christ? Shall tribulation, or distress, or persecution, or famine, or nakedness, or peril, or sword? As it is written, For thy sake we are killed all the day long; we are accounted as sheep for the slaughter. Nay, in all these things, we are more than conquerors through him that loved us.

For I am persuaded, that neither death, nor life, nor angels, nor principalities, nor powers, nor things present, nor things to come, Nor height, nor depth, nor any creature, shall be able to separate us from the love of God, which is in Christ Jesus our Lord.

To God be the glory for giving us his words to strengthen and encourage us always. The Holy Bible is a storehouse of spiritual nourishment, and the shelves will never go or look empty, no matter how much of it is being digested. Suppose the children of God continue to feast on this nourishment. In that case, they will allow us to grow strong so that we, with the help of the Holy Spirit, will resist and push back the advancing of the evil one who is here only to steal, kill spiritually, and destroy the inner spirit of anyone that he can.

The enemy of God does not want to see all the praises that are going up to our Father in heaven. He will try as much as he can to mess up anyone's inner spirit that he can because a destroyed inner spirit will have many problems producing praise. The enemy of God was also possessed with this jealous mentality when he was residing in heaven, and his name was Lucifer. He held a very high-level position. He developed something within himself that produced a sin-like condition not allowed there in heaven and was expelled with all his followers.

Jesus desired that his church, which are all the people that had and will ask him to come into their hearts and lives and be their Lord to love one another, help each other, and be on one accord as the disciples were on the day of Pentecost when the Holy Spirit came to us. Think of how beautiful and lovely the praises sometimes are and should always be when everyone who walked through the church's doors came to worship God and were all on one accord sincerely making a joyful noise.

King David said in Psalm 84:4–5, "Blessed are they that dwell in thy house: they will be still praising thee. Blessed is the man whose strength is in thee; in whose heart are the ways of them." Please understand, my sisters and brothers in Christ, that many blessings are being poured out on us while we are praising our heavenly Father in the name of Jesus, our Lord and Savior.

Every person born on this planet is blessed in each individual way, and we are all created to glorify and praise God. Over one hundred scriptures testify to the evidence of that statement, from the president on down to the person sweeping the street, the person sitting in a wheelchair, or even all the others dealing with all kinds of situations. No matter where you are in life or what the situations might be that you are experiencing, everyone should give God thanks that the day you were born, God allows you to breathe the outstanding and excellent air that he has made to fuel our earthly existence.

Many generations have come, lived, and had their own individual life experiences and then exited the earth to another place. Here we are in this time, a very perilous and troublesome period of time, but

King Soloman once made a statement that there is nothing new under the sun.

So all the generations before us were probably thinking the same thing as we are thinking now because ever since Adam and Eve disobeyed their Creator, because of the influence of Satan through the serpent, they were put out of the garden of Eden. Satan was also expelled out of heaven along with his other angel's conspirators, now called demons. Trouble has been plaguing the earth.

Since the creation of humans, we also know that all the generations did not experience the Redeemer in the way that we are all blessed to call upon his name now in our time. Christ Jesus had come to save us just two thousand-plus years ago, although he had always been in heaven with his Father, waiting on the time that the Father would allow him to come. According to scientists, humans have been on the earth for between five and seven million years. Wow, that is a long time.

The understanding is that all those people that have exited the earth had to wait in another place for Jesus to come and give his life as a sacrifice, dying on the cross to conquer death, to be the one to be resurrected and return to the Father in heaven, so that in the resurrection and judgment that is to come, people who have died long ago based on the chosen of the heavenly host will answer to whatever the wrong deed they had committed.

The people of God now, who are sold out to Christ and with the help of the Holy Spirit, are pressing on in righteousness, keeping clean hands, and being pure in their hearts with the help from above. They will not see death in the same way as those long-ago generations before Christ. That is the promise of Jesus, and we can trust in his word.

That in itself deserved a multitude of praise, to depart the painful fleshly body and be renewed instantly in a spiritual body. The thought of it makes me want to step away from my typewriter and dance and praise God. Hello, my readers, that is what I did. I was filled with thanksgiving that I had to step away to give God the glory and praise him.

I was probably feeling a little of what the man of praises felt, no other than King David in the book of Psalm. Let us reflect on Psalm 150:1–6.

> PRAISE YE the Lord. Praise God in his sanctuary: praise him in the firmament of his power. Praise him for his mighty acts; praise him according to his excellent greatness. Praise him with the sound of the trumpet: praise him with the psaltery and harp. Praise him with the timbrel and dance: praise him with stringed instruments and organs. Praise him upon the loud cymbals: praise him upon the high sounding cymbals. Let every thing that hath breath praise the Lord. Praise ye the Lord.

After over fifty years of preaching and teaching, I declare now to all my readers, by the power and inspiration of the Holy Spirit given to me, that no one has to wait until Sunday in the church to praise God. Wherever you are, as long as it is safe and you will not hurt yourself, praise your God when the feelings hit you. No company or crowd is required to praise. Sometimes more sincere praises come upon you when you are alone, and if you are listening to gospel music on the radio or computer, dance for the Lord. Our God loves to see a joyful inner spirit in his children.

King David once said, "I was happy when they said unto me, let us go into the house of the Lord." When any of us people of God truly think of the goodness of God the Father, God the Son, and God the Holy Spirit and all that has been done for us, we should be stirred up in our heart and inner spirit to just want to praise. This is the mentality that all people of God should have when entering the house of worship. The word (not quoted) is entered into my gate with thanksgiving and into the courts with praise. Be thankful unto him and bless his name for the Lord is good and his mercy endured to all generations.

In these troublesome times we are living in, when it is a good thing to pray before leaving home, say goodbye to the loved ones in the morning, never knowing if returning home will be granted. When we make it back home, don't forget to thank you, Father God, in the name of Jesus because so many have left home in the mornings and never made it back home to their loving family.

There are so many hurting families worldwide because of the loss of their loved ones. We need to stop taking life and things that God has provided for us on this planet for granted. No one knows the minute or hour when their name will be called to give up the flesh and be transitioned to a spiritual body. Brothers and sisters, let us all be ready like the five wise virgins who trimmed their lamps and made sure they had additional oil for the waiting journey. The words of God are our oil. Please let us all study the words of God as often as we can, and the Holy Spirit of God will help us along our life journey in the name of Jesus.

8

Let Not Your Heart Be Troubled

Those words were from Jesus, the Son of God, one of the three-part of the Trinity that you can put all your trust in his hands. He was speaking to his disciples in preparation for returning to his heavenly Father. Jesus knew what was in their hearts, and like the best shepherd that ever walked on this Earth, Jesus was preparing them, as he though the written and inspired Bible were preparing us for his return.

John 14:1–3 reads,

> LET NOT your heart be troubled: ye believe in God, believe also in me. In my Father's house are many mansions: if it were not so, I would have told you. I go to prepare a place for you. And if I go and prepare a place for you, I will come again, and receive you unto myself; that where I am, there ye may be also.

My sisters and brothers in Christ, with spiritual discernment, let us truly reflect on these verses of Jesus's statement. First of all, as always, Jesus emphasizes belief, which is the foundation of faith. Believing in him comes before faith in him. Jesus is saying here that if you truly believe that there is a God and you believe in what the God you believe in says to you, that God so loved the world, that he gave his only begotten Son, and that whosoever believeth in him should not perish but have everlasting life.

If you truly in your heart believe that I am the Son of God, then please believe in what I am going to tell you, just as how you believe in God the Father. If you believe that in the beginning was the Word and the Word was with God and that the Word was God, the same was in the beginning with God. He was a part of the process of all things made, and without him was not anything made that was made. In him was life, and the life was the light of men. Although these other statements were written by the disciples long after Jesus made his statement, for us, we can discern that Jesus wants to allow (believing) to be understood by them and even us today.

If we pay close attention to our Bible reading, we will notice that Jesus did not promise them that after he was gone, he was going to use his power to let each of them get a condo to live in and many other earthly things. Most of us humans worldwide would like to get all our blessings here on earth. Our earthly life is all we know, and so when Jesus told them that they should not let their hearts be troubled, most likely they were listening for his next statement to be more like giving them something they could get and enjoy here on earth while he was gone.

Jesus was more concerned about their everlasting life situation than the temporary earthly life that every human will live for the time allocated to each one. Jesus also knows that the earth was created and designed to provide for everyone and everything that allowed them to live there. The earth automatically provides from the depth of the great ocean to the flying creature in the skies. The words of Jesus are sometimes not digested enough. They are not being pondered as they should. When Jesus spoke to them then, he also was speaking for many generations to come into existence.

Please, let us take time now to read what Jesus again said to his disciples in Matthew 6:25–34. Please remember as you read this book that the inspired words of the Bible are the foundation from which my inspiration derives and not from earthly memoirs. I am inspired to teach the truth of God's words and to help as many as the Holy Spirit will use these books to repair, renew, reinspired, refresh, reinvigorate, and regenerate a newness in every reader's inner spirit and heart. To be more determined to stay on the narrow path that will lead them into the kingdom of God, I only ask the Holy Spirit to allow me to be the conduit to as many as he chooses.

> Therefore I say unto you, take no thought for your life, what shall we eat, or what ye shall drink; nor yet for your body, what ye shall put on. Is not the life more than the meat? Behold the fowls of the air: for they sow not, neither do they reap, nor gather into barns; yet your Heavenly Father feedeth them. Are ye not much better than they?

> Which of you by taking thought can add one cubit unto his stature? And why take ye thought for raiment? Consider the lilies of the field, how they grow; they toil not, neither do they spin: And yet I say unto you, That even Soloman in all his Glory was not arrayed like one of these.

> Wherefore, if God so clothe the grass of the field, which today is, and tomorrow is cast into the oven, shall he not much more clothe you, O ye of little faith?

> Therefore take no thought, saying, What shall I eat? or, What shall we drink? or, Wherewithal shall

we be clothed? (For after all these things do the Gentiles seek:) for your Heavenly Father knoweth that ye have need of all these things.

But seek ye first the Kingdom of God, and his righteousness; and all these things shall be added unto you. Take therefore no thought for the morrow: for the morrow shall take thought for the things of itself. Sufficient unto the day is the evil thereof.

When Jesus speaks, blessed are they that have been blessed with a spiritual heart to hear and the gift of understanding to ponder and digest his words and see that Jesus is not saying that we do not need earthly sustenances to live a good life. But we lack faith, so we tend to worry about things that will happen anyway, even if we did not worry about it.

Jesus in all his earthly ministries tried to help us understand the importance of faith. People carry their concerns, problems, and bad feelings to the altar in their church because of the urging of the pastor to bring them and leave them there, but because of the lack of faith when they go home, they realize they had brought what should have been left at the altar back to their seat and now back home with them.

Because of the concerns of earthly needs, which Jesus says that our heavenly Father already knows about, he will allow us to get the needed things of life so we can focus on the kingdom of heaven where all of our focus should be by leaving everything in God's hands. Instead people worry about tomorrow, forgetting the good that God had done for them yesterday.

The readers of this book will be most likely more adult than children if we reflect on our lives and understand that the same God who had cared for us even as an infant and even further back in our mother's womb is the same loving God that is going to care for us for as long as we are on this planet, and our memory will help us keep our focus on seeking first the kingdom of heaven.

Heaven help us all. Holy Spirit, in the name of Jesus, please help us in increasing our faith. Let not your heart be troubled because there is nothing on this planet or anywhere in the universe that God cannot fix. Jesus desires for our focus to be more on the everlasting life that we will inherit, more than putting most of our focus on this temporary life here on earth. The place is already prepared for all of God's children. Jesus did everything his heavenly Father had assigned him to bring us home, where we will praise him day and night forever.

There is and should be a difference between the people of God and the people of the world in the way the things of the world are viewed. That is why Jesus said in verse 32, "For after all these things do the Gentiles seek: for your Heavenly Father knoweth that ye have need of all these things." The Gentiles is a reference to the people of the world whose hearts and minds are not on heavenly things but are drowned in earthly desires and wants, temporary greeds that will not even travel with no one's accumulation to the grave.

As children of the Most High God, we should never miss the sight of what God has been and is still doing for us. If one door is closed, God already knew it was going to be closed way ahead of time and has already prepared another door that will open to you. When Jesus was ready to go to Jerusalem, he told two of his disciples to go and get a donkey at a specific place. How did Jesus know that the donkey would be there? Because the heavenly powers know all things and can fix all things according to the Father's will ahead of time. The heavenly powers know what tomorrow or two thousand years from now will bring, and yet we do not have enough faith to trust God with tomorrow's provision. In this world that we live in, people have to see with their physical eyes to believe.

Let us reflect on this awesome time when Jesus knew that his earthly mission was coming to an end and that there were certain things he had to do for the fulfillment of why he came. Mark 11:1–11 reads,

AND WHEN they came nigh to Jerusalem, unto Bethphage and Bethany, at the Mount of Olives, he sendeth forth two of his disciples, And saith unto them, Go your way into the village over against you: and as soon as ye be entered into it, ye shall find a colt tied, whereon never man sat; loose him, and bring him,

And if any man say unto you, why do ye this? say ye that the Lord hath need of him; and straightway he will send him hither. And they went their way, and found the colt tied by the door without in a place where two ways met; and they loose him. And certain of them that stood there said unto them, What do ye, loosing the colt? And they said unto them even as Jesus had commanded: and they let them go. And they brought the colt to Jesus, and cast their garments on him; and he sat upon him.

And many spread their garments in the way: and others cut down branches off the trees, and strawed them in the way. And they that went before, and they that followed, cried, saying, Hosanna; Blessed is he that cometh in the name of the Lord: Blessed be the kingdom of our Father David, that cometh in the name of the Lord: Hosanna in the highest. And Jesus entered into Jerusalem, and into the temple: and when he had looked round about upon all things, and now the eventide was come, he went out unto Bethany with the twelve.

Let not your heart be troubled because Jesus walks the talk. Jesus was God the Son, with a fleshly body surrounding an enormous spiritual power that no one could see. Only through the miracles he performed did these powers of God reveal themselves, like when Jesus came into Jericho. Let's read what happens there. Mark 10:46–52 reads,

> And they came to Jericho: and as he went out of Jericho with his disciples and a great number of people, blind Bartimaeus, the son of Timaeus, sat by the highway side begging. And when he heard that it was Jesus of Nazareth, he began to cry out, and say, Jesus, thou son of David, have mercy on me.
>
> And many charged him that he should hold his peace: but he cried the more a great deal, Thou son of David, have mercy on me. And Jesus stood still, and commanded him to be called. And they call the blind man, saying unto him, Be of good comfort, rise; he calleth thee. And he, casting away his garment, rose, and came to Jesus. And Jesus answered and said unto him, What wilt thou that I should do unto thee? The blind man said unto him, Lord, that I might receive my sight. And Jesus said unto him, Go thy way; thy faith hath made thee whole. And immediately he received his sight, and followed Jesus in the way.

Hallelujah, Hallelujah, Hallelujah to our most holy and wise everlasting God. Thank you, heavenly Father, for sending your only begotten Son to heal and save us so we can come into your kingdom at the appointed time. We will give up the trapping of the fleshly body that cannot enter into the kingdom of heaven and set our inner spirit free to come to you. Thank you, Father, for the help of your Holy Spirit that is guiding and leading us while we are traveling the dark road of life that without the light of Jesus, we all would not be able to see your love for us and what is ahead.

While Jesus was here in the flesh, only a partial nugget of heavenly power could be contained within the fleshly body, although he could summon any amount of heavenly powers he needed. So please allow your spiritual imagination to envision Jesus now at his heavenly Father's right hand with all the powers of heaven that he had and was used to, all given back to him. And if when he were here with us, people who had enough faith drew the power of healing from him, how much more we in this generation should be drawing from the heavenly host through faith in the person of the Holy Spirit.

Jesus, Jesus, is the most powerful name that I know. I encourage all my Christian brothers and sisters to be continuously mindful and aware that this heavenly power-filled Jesus loves us just like his Father God does. There should be nothing in this temporary physical and sinful world that should keep the children of God from not pressing on with increased determination and with the help of the Holy Spirit to walk through heaven's gate in the new spiritual body seeing Jesus face-to-face. Oh, what a joy-filled day that will be when all the saints of God gather around God's throne. Those who have persevered through the struggle of their earthly existence choose Jesus as their Savior and stay in their lane of righteousness, refusing to allow the cunning, evil, and mischievous enemy of God, Satan, to deceive them.

Jesus, who is God the Son, had all the pleasure it did bring him doing his heavenly Father's will, and if we remember the day that John baptized him in the River Jordon as an example for us to follow, on that day, the heavens were opened unto him, and he saw the Holy Spirit of his Father descending in the form of a dove and lighting upon him. There was a voice from heaven in which his heavenly Father said, "This is my beloved Son, in whom I am well, pleased, Jesus." Heavenly Father was able to say how proud he was of his Son because his Son was obedient and his only desire was to please his Father, not like sons who want to take their Father's position.

Let us read what Jesus's blessings of obedience are in Philippians 2:5–13, and I pray that the Holy Spirit will guide all our hearts to desire to walk in the examples of the one that will take us through heaven's gate.

> Let this mind be in you, which was also in Christ Jesus: Who, being in the form of God, thought it not robbery to be equal with God: But made himself of no reputation, and took upon him the form of a servant, and was made in the likeness of men: And being found in fashion as a man, he humbled himself, and became obedient unto death, even the death of the cross.

> Wherefore God also hath highly exalted him, and given him a name which is above every name: That at the name of Jesus every knee should bow, of things in Heaven, and things in Earth, and things under the Earth; And that every tongue should confess that Jesus Christ is Lord, to the Glory of God the Father. Wherefore, my beloved, as ye have always obeyed, not as in my presence only, but now much more in my absence, work out your own salvation with fear and trembling. For it is God which worketh in you both to will and to do of his good pleasure.

Please note this statement of the apostle Paul, speaking to the church there in Philippi and us even now (work out your own salvation with fear and trembling). The inspired Paul is stressing to us—and I am sure in his heart he is hoping—that we get the understanding that none of the children of God should live their Christian lives focusing on what others are doing wrong. Many Christians get discouraged because others, even those we seem to look up to, believe they are spiritually strong when they fall along the wayside through the lust of worldly desires. If we are not mindful, it can be very discouraging.

Like a Christian father who had his share of worldliness, Paul, as we all know from whence, he came. We also know that what we had done before we met Christ is automatically forgiven. But as Jesus told the young lady he spared from getting stoned to death for her misgivings (go and sin no more), there is hardly anyone who can throw stones at somebody else as if they were always a saint. If we should be honest, as we will in this context, everybody dilly-dallies at some time in their life before they met Christ. That is why Jesus told Mr. Nicodemus that day, "You must be born again," spiritually speaking, of course, as Jesus explained to him.

Many people go through the whole process, and some have a good and sincere intention of working with their feelings and changing their lives. Jesus told a parable, which I will use as an example about the sower that sow the seeds that fell on stony ground.

> … who, when they have heard the word, immediately receive it with gladness; And have no root in themselves, and so endure but for a time: afterward, when affliction or persecution ariseth for the word's sake, immediately they are offended. (Matthew 13:16–17)

So be mindful of what Paul is saying in his statement of working out your own salvation with fear and trembling because each of us as Christians has to stand on our own two feet with the help of the Holy Spirit. You cannot be righteous for another person or someone else being righteous for you. Each of our hearts is the soil in which the seed of the heavenly kingdom is planted.

So we need to examine ourselves and be determined to allow the principles and laws of God to take root deep within us so we can bear good fruits in righteousness. Help as many as you can along the Christian journey, and those who do not want to be helped, please do not allow them to discourage you, whether they are family members, friends, coworkers, or even spouses. You need to press on as you continue to pray for them and keep your focus on Christ.

"Heaven help us all" has to be the continuous prayer. Let not your heart be troubled. Anyone worldwide—skin color, language, culture, size, residence, health, or fitness—has nothing to do with it. It does not matter who you are or what you had done in your life before you met Jesus. All of us—that is, everyone who accepts Jesus as the Son of God, the Creator, and asks him sincerely to be the ruler of their life and are willing to be born again from the sinful mindset to a spiritual mindset and walk in the Spirit of righteousness—will be in line for the same blessing of everlasting life.

Prayer is to be used as the walking cane for every Christian. Prayer is what we have to lean on, and as everyone knows by now, we are living in a time when communication with your heavenly Father is so essential that the minimum of daily prayer should be at least morning, noon, and night. And if we feel the need to squeeze more in between, our loving God will never get tired of hearing from us.

God knows that the more a person prays, the more spiritually uplifting feelings will be generated. Remember, God used to go to see about Adam very often and hear all the details of what he was naming all the earthly creatures and all the other concerns he might have had. Communication between God and man was at its highest peak until we all knew what had happened.

That most precious godly link was broken, but thanks to our loving Lord and Savior, Jesus Christ, the repair has been done, and the communication link is back up and will always stay strong for all God's people worldwide. To God the Father be all the honor, praise, and glory forever in the mighty name of God the Son, Jesus. We need to spend more time on the spiritual line than on the cell phone line. No one down here on this planet can pay your way into heaven, even if you spend all day or night on the phone with the pastor or first lady.

They cannot help you as the Holy Spirit can, and they might need to get on the spiritual phone line themselves. Please remember, sisters and brothers, that the Holy Spirit is the administrator, overseer, and headmaster of the church, and wherever the Holy Spirit resides, God the Father and God the Son are also there in Spirit. There is nothing on this earth to compare to the heavenly Trinity of three-in-one.

Let not your heart be troubled because the heavenly Trinity will help us until it is time to go home, each in their own time. And heaven will not run out of room, like it was at Jesus's birth where no room was in the inn. Jesus called it as he knew it when he said, "In my Father's house, there are many mansions." We just need to focus on the righteous path that will lead us to this unimaginable place, never seen by any human being in the flesh since creation.

But hold on, my brothers and sisters in Christ, be strong in the faith that God has blessed us with because every one of God's people is going to be faced with some kind of problem and situation to deal with as long as we are here on this earth. The spiritual warfare is very real and strong; God's enemy is attacking his people from a place of lofty heights, but we know that he will lose the battle in the mighty name of Jesus.

One day at a time, dear Jesus, please help us to make it one day at a time. The statement of "Let not your heart be troubled" was not based on a concept I dream about in the middle of the night. As all Christians should, I study the word of God to show myself approved. I feast on the spiritual nourishment of God's words, and that is why my encouragement to you, the readers, is totally grounded in the Bible.

When you are reading a book, the author often mentions scripture that you might not be able to view from the Bible at that time. So you kind of miss out on the good feelings of the scripture right then. That is why as you read this book, you can also read the quoted scriptures as if we are all studying together in the name of Jesus.

Jesus is the door to the heavenly kingdom, and because we are followers of Jesus when we read the New Testament, the greater emphasis should be on what Jesus said. We should truly ponder his words because they are full of truth and wisdom above all that King Soloman had. Jesus is God the Son. His coming to earth was not for a joyride from out of the great unknown. He was here on a mission to save humans.

Jesus spoke words of healing, encouragement, comfort, and chastizement, and he lived his life in righteousness, with his focus on his heavenly Father, and did all he was assigned to do before going home to his heavenly Father. It is too much for us here on earth to even imagine what the heavenly atmosphere was like when he walked back in and stood at the throne of God the Father.

Let us, please, reflect on these words of Jesus that he spoke and ponder the deep wisdom in all of them on a day when he healed a multitude of people. Luke 6:17–49 reads,

> And he came down with them, and stood in the plain, and the company of his disciples, and great multitude of people out of all Judaea and Jerusalem, and from the sea coast of Tyre and Sidon, which came to hear him, and to be healed of their diseases; And they that were vexed with unclean spirits: and they were healed. And the whole multitude sought to touch him: for there went virtue out of him, and healed them all.
>
> And he lifted up his eyes on his disciples, and said, Blessed be ye poor: for yours is the kingdom of God. Blessed are ye that hunger now: for ye shall be filled. Blessed are ye that weep now: for ye shall laugh. Blessed are ye, when men shall hate you, and when they shall separate you from their company, and shall reproach you, and cast out your name as evil,

121

for the Son of man's sake. Rejoice ye in that day, and leap for joy: for, behold, your reward is great in heaven: for in the like manner did their fathers unto the prophets.

But who unto you that are rich! for ye have received your consolation. Who unto you that are full! for ye shall be hunger. Who unto you that laugh now! for ye shall mourn and weep. Who unto you, when all men shall speak well of you! for so did their fathers to the false prophets. But I say unto you which hear, love your enemies, do good to them which hate you. Bless them that curse you, and pray for them which despitefully use you.

And unto him that smiteth thee on the one cheek offer also the other; and him that taketh away thy cloak forbid not to take thy coat also. Give to every man that asketh of thee; and of him that taketh away thy goods ask them not again. And as ye would that men should do to you, do ye also to them likewise. For if ye love them which love you, what thank have ye? for sinners also love those that love them. And if ye do good to them which do good to you, what thank have ye? for sinners also do even the same.

And if ye lend to them of whom ye hope to receive, what thank have ye? for sinners also lend to sinners, to receive as much again. But love ye your enemies, and do good, and lend, hoping for nothing again; and your reward shall be great, and ye shall be the children of the Highest: for he is kind unto the unthankful and to the evil. Be ye therefore merciful, as your Father also is merciful. Judge not, and ye shall not be judged: condemn not, and ye shall not be condemned: forgive, and ye shall be forgiven: Give, and it shall be given unto you; good maesure, pressed down, and shaken together, and running over, shall men give into your bosom. For with the same measure that ye mete withal it shall be measured to you again.

As followers of Jesus, we should not pick and choose what we want to hear from him. How much he loves us and what he is going to give us should not be the only words that should impress us as Christians. If we just do what the world does, how different are we from them is what Jesus is trying to let us understand. Jesus said that his heavenly Father is kind unto the unthankful and to the evil because he is merciful. Therefore, if we are his children, then we also have to be merciful, and when bad-minded people go low, as Christians, we have to go high, staying on the high and righteous side of the situation. Jesus used the word *blessed*, for everything that is not easy to do generates a blessing.

It takes a lot more than looking good in church on Sundays to walk the road of righteousness. Read from the Bible the words that feel like they are stepping on your toes, for that also generates blessings as we will bear more spiritual fruits and be able to draw more souls into God's kingdom the way we live our daily lives at home, or on the job, or even in the supermarket.

As Christians, we are always on the narrow road that leads to our heavenly Father, no matter where we are, and also remember that Satan and his demons are keeping one eye on all followers of Jesus to make you look bad and get discouraged every chance they get. In the precious and majestic name of Jesus, thanks will always be to God for sending his Holy Spirit, and if we walk with him in the Spirit, no weapon formed against us will ever prosper. To God be the glory forever and ever. Amen. Let not your heart be troubled.

9

God's Desires and His Will Must Be Done

"And God said, Let there be light: and there was light" (Genesis 1:3). "And God said, Let the Earth bring forth grass, the herb yielding seed, and the fruit tree yielding fruit after his kind, whose seed is in itself, upon the Earth: and it was so" (Genesis 1:11). "And God said, Let the Earth bring forth the living creature after his kind, cattle, and creeping thing, and beast of the Earth after his kind: and it was so" (Genesis 1:24).

And here is where we humans began. Genesis 1:26–30 reads,

> And God said, Let us make man in our image, after our likeness: and let them have dominion over the fish of the sea, and over the fowl of the air, and over the cattle, and over all the earth, and over every creeping thing that creepeth upon the earth.

So God created man in his own image, in the image God created he him; male and female created he them. And God blessed them, and God said unto them, Be fruitful, and multiply, and replenish the Earth, and subdue it: and have dominion over the fish of the sea, and over the fowl of the air, and over every living thing that moveth upon the Earth.

And God said, Behold, I have given you every herb bearing seed, which is upon the face of all the Earth, and every tree, in the which is the fruit of a tree yielding seed; to you it shall be for meat. And to every beast of the Earth, and to every fowl of the air, and to every thing that creepeth upon the Earth, wherein there is life, I have given every green herb for meat: and it was so. And God saw everything that he had made, and, behold, it was very good. And the evening and the morning were the sixth day.

To God be the glory forever and ever. The Bible so eloquently explains to us that God saw everything that he had made, and behold, it was very good. Please reflect on this, that God's creation was not just good, but very good. When we use the word *very*, that means whatever very is referring to is more than just good. Scientists have used these variations to create a more reliable molecular clock and found that Adam lived between 120,000 and 156,000 years ago. A comparable analysis of the same men's sequences suggested that Eve lived between 99,000 and 148,000 years ago.

Scientists also estimated the Earth to be 4.54 billion years old, plus or minus about 50 million years. Scientists have scoured the Earth, searching for the oldest rocks to date radiometrically. It is said that approximately 300,000 years ago, the first Homo sapiens, that is, anatomically modern humans, arose alongside our other hominid relatives. And when we research how long a day was 4 billion years ago, the research shows that days on earth are getting longer due to the moon's effect on our planet's rotation. 1.4 billion years ago, the moon was a bit closer, and the Earth's rotation was faster, which let a day on earth be just over eighteen hours. On average, we gain 0.00001542857 seconds a year.

The scientific community will never stop exploring because of the astonishing findings in the awesomeness of God's creation. And while they are being baffled over there, we, the Christian community, are just giving our awesome God the honor, glory, and praises for his creation. It is amazing how manufactured stuff by man does not last too long. Look how long ago the sun is shining for us after the day arrives, and the moon has always been there to help us at night in so many ways. God's fruit trees are still bearing fruits, and how beautiful is the green vegetation that is a blessing to all humans. The most healthy food comes from the earth.

God said, "And it was so." Let us look at Genesis 2:7–9.

> And the Lord God formed man of the dust of the ground, and breathed into his nostrils the breath of life; and the man became a living soul. And the Lord God planted a garden eastward in Eden; and there he put the man whom he had formed. And out of the ground made the Lord God to grow every tree that is pleasant to the sight, and good for food; the tree of life; and the tree of knowledge of good and evil.

When I ponder deeply and give attention to this one tree of two parts or two sides, I reflect on the entire creation of the universe as in two parts also: good and evil, positive and negative, sun and moon, day and night, male and female, hot and cold, fire and water, and on and on. Let's look at positive and negative. We view positively as good and negatively as bad. But when you reflect on electricity, there would be no light with just positive alone and no light with negative alone. We need them both for the modern technological life we have been living. Positive and negative are on the same tree.

When we reflect on the Tree of Knowledge of Good and Evil, the word *knowledge* has to be emphasized. With this tree, we get the knowledge of whether something is good or evil, which seems to be the system that allows humans to have the freedom of choice. And although the word *evil* is mentioned in Genesis 1:31, it reads, "And God saw everything that he had made, and, behold, it was very good." That tree was not placed there in the middle of the garden by accident; it was put there for a reason, of which we will never know because the Bible has not really elaborated on it except they were not supposed to eat from it, maybe until an appointed time.

Whatever the reason is, God desires things to be the way it is, and it was so. We humans are full of speculations on just about every subject, even those many things about the creation and the universe that we do not understand. Thanks to technology, scientists are always searching and digging to come up with their own speculation, as they did with the big bang theory of how the Earth was formed. By faith in the words of God, the people of God rest their case on the Genesis creation story and leave everything else in God's hands. Let God's will be done, not that we have a choice in the matter.

People have tried to run away from the calling to service by God, and their results were not something very happy to write home about. Jonah's story of trying to evade and hide from the mission that God wanted him to do will be told in many generations to come, if that is God's will for it to be so and he will grant the time.

Bible prophecy fulfillment is at its max in these troublesome times, and no man knows the minute or the hour when God the Father will give God the Son the nod that it is time as Jesus is patiently waiting so he can return to get his church that is very dear to him. Jesus's church is his faithful and righteous followers, not the beautiful church buildings that many are hiding in playing around with Christianity.

God has desired many changes since creation. God desires to make a change, and so he prepared a man named Noah to go to work, which he did, and saved himself and his family. Genesis 7:1 reads, "AND THE Lord said unto Noah, Come thou and all thy house into the ark; for thee have I seen righteous before me in this generation." Our loving God desires for Abram to be prepared for a certain mission. He told him to get out of his country and from his kindred and his father's house unto a land that would be shown to him.

His wife, Sarai, probably thought that her husband made some more tea from that plant she did not like him to drink and was talking funny when he told her what God said to do and wanted her to go with him when he did not even know where they were going. Still, blessed are all wives who know that they have a good husband and will step out on faith with him.

God is still working through righteous people, and even those who may not be ready but have the heart to adjust to God's will, he can clean them up if that is his desire and use them. Jacob was twisted and definitely not ready, but God desired to use him, so God fixed him up over time to meet the mission in God's heart for him. God had a mission for Joseph, so he had to be put in the right place and position, so he ended up in Egypt through some not-very-nice experiences, but God was always with him and caused him to be a prosperous man. When God's favor is on you, no person can block the blessings of God on your life. Who God blesses, no man can curse.

Let us not forget about our brother Moses. It seems that God had the desire to choose him from birth or even before he was born and in his mother's womb. Grace, mercy, and the favor of God were on his life. Because of his mother's plight, this little guy was put in a basket as a baby and set sail down the river without a paddle. Still, all along, God knew how everything in his life was going to work out, and he ended up growing up in the right house. The daughter of Pharoah was already chosen to retrieve him from the river.

And amazingly, the same mother that put him to sail was hired to be his caretaker. When the appointed time had come for his mission to start, he had to run away from all the comfort he had to begin the assignment of eventually bringing the children of Israel, who was the same Jacob that an angel changed his name, out of bondage in Egypt. The power of God is amazing; to him be all the glory.

Our loving heavenly Father has chosen people in all generations to be put in place so that his desire can be done. To help the Israelites, his chosen people, he had selected a beautiful lady named Ruth from a peculiar situation to save God's people at the appointed time. Ruth and her husband, Elimelech, had two sons and lived in Moab. Sometime later, Elimelech, Naomi's husband, died. She was left with her two sons, Mahlon and Chilion. Mahlon married a woman named Orpah, and Chilion married beautiful Ruth. Some years later, both of these husbands died, and so Naomi was just left with her two daughters-in-law.

Naomi encouraged these two ladies just to go back to their people, and Orpah eventually returned, but Ruth decided to stay with her and be a help to her grieving mother-in-law because Ruth had a good and compassionate heart because God had already chosen her for a mission even though she had problems in her life. Through the amazing works of God, Ruth married again to a king and became a queen, and she was in a position to help the people of God. Hallelujah to his name. As Christians, we have to reflect on the awesome working of God with humans down through the many generations. God had never abandoned his human creation. That is why when the appointed time came, Jesus was here for us now to be saved.

Hallelujah, Hallelujah, to God's Holy Name. Honor, glory, and praise should always be given to our heavenly Father and Creator. The love God has for his human creation is not easy for us to comprehend. That is why we have embraced John 3:16–17 with all our hearts. "For God so loved the world, that he gave his only begotten Son, that whosoever believeth in him should not perish, but have everlasting life. For God sent not his Son into the world to condemn the world; but that the world through him might be saved."

Let us reflect on a few more people from the past that our loving God used to move forward with his desires. How can we not speak concerning Samuel? His mother was told that she could not have any children. It was said the Lord had shut up her womb. Because humans do not know the heart of God and what his desires will be, our heavenly Father used this same womb that people thought would be closed for good to bring forth a handsome and godly man named Samuel who became a priest because of God's calling on his life.

Samuel was used to anoint the first king of Israel, Saul. God eventually removed King Saul because of his misdeeds, and David became king over the people of Israel and reigned over Judah for seven years in Hebron and then Israel and Judah in Jerusalem for thirty-three years, forty years in total. This same David had an exciting life experience but is very much reflected on in the book of Psalm, which brings comfort and hopes to many.

God has brought about 124,000 prophets in total throughout history. However, the five books of the major prophets are Isaiah, Jeremiah, Lamentation, Ezekiel, and Daniel. Isaiah spoke to the nation of Judah about 150 years before their exile into Babylonia and called them to be faithful to God. Let's reflect on Jeremiah for a little while. Jeremiah's ministry covered the period just before and after the fall of Jerusalem in 587 BC. Jeremiah warned the Jews that God would send the Babylonian armies to punish Jerusalem's ungodliness for many years. His continuing emphasis on approaching doom made him very unpopular, hated by kings, princes, priests, other prophets, and citizens.

During the final siege of Jerusalem, he was imprisoned as a traitor for advising Jerusalem not to resist the Babylonian soldiers. After the fall of Jerusalem, Jeremiah accompanied some fleeing Jews to Egypt, where he continued his faithful proclamation of God's

Word until he died in obscurity. He lived his life doing the will of God, which all the called people of God should do. Please take your time to ponder when God called young Jeremiah. God is still calling people to his kingdom service, and there are no differences in the wages. Every faithful worker gets the same promise of everlasting life.

Jeremiah 1:5–9 reads,

> Before I formed thee in the belly I knew thee; and before thou camest forth out of the womb I sanctified thee, and I ordained thee a prophet unto the nations. Then said I, Ah, Lord God! behold, I cannot speak: for I am a child. But the Lord said unto me, Say not, I am a child: for thou shalt go to all that I shall send thee, and whatsoever I command thee thou shalt speak. Be not afraid of their faces: for I am with thee to deliver thee, saith the Lord. Then the Lord put forth his hand, and touched my mouth. And the Lord said unto me, Behold, I have put my words in thy mouth.

Brothers and sisters in Christ, please remember that God has been using people as a blessing to others, and likewise, Satan is also using people to deceive others. The Bible said, "By the fruit, you shall know them." As for us as Christians and followers of Christ Jesus, we are and should produce the fruits of the Spirit.

Jeremiah had a big ministry to accomplish, but God is so loving and faithful, and his grace and mercy are so much more than we can even comprehend. God had done so much for his people then, and generation after generation was so ungrateful and allowed the things of the world through other cultures and greed to corrupt their hearts. They were not able to stay spiritual as they had begun depending on the God of Abraham, Isaac, and Jacob.

It was a very troublesome time that Jeremiah had to work in, but he kept the faith and did what the Lord had assigned him to do. Let us reflect on Jeremiah 3:20–25.

> Surely as a wife treacherously departeth from her husband, so have ye dealt treacherously with me, O house of Israel, saith the Lord. A voice was heard upon the high places, weeping, and supplications of the children of Israel: for they have perverted their way, and they have forgotten the Lord their God.

> Truly in vain is salvation hoped for from the hills, and from the multitude of mountains: truly in the Lord our God is the salvation of Israel. For shame hath devoured the labour of our fathers from youth; their flocks and their herds, their sons, and their daughters. We lie down in our shame, and our confusion covereth us: for we have sinned against the Lord our God, we and our fathers, from our youth even unto this day, and have not obeyed the voice of the Lord our God.

Listen now to what the merciful God told them through Jeremiah in 4:1–2, "IF THOU wilt return, O Israel, saith the Lord, return unto me: and if thou will put away thine abominations out of my sight, then shalt thou not remove. And thou shalt swear, The Lord liveth, in truth, in judgment, and in righteousness; and the nations shall bless themselves in him, and in him shall they Glory."

Hallelujah to your most Holy Name, O God, for you desire for none to be lost if they would just repent and turn from their evil ways and the fleshly lust of the world. The same message from Jeremiah is still alive and well even now in the time we are living. Some people are living their lives as if anything goes, and God is not watching or caring about what humans do anymore. That is why Jesus will separate the sheep from the goats, and Jesus knows his sheep. The wheat and the tears will grow until the day of harvest.

Jesus also knows the wolves in sheep's clothing because people can fool others sometimes, but no one on this Planet Earth can fool or hide from God at no time. People are only fooling themselves. We have to always remember that when this fleshly body is vacated, there is more than one direction that the spirit can travel, heaven or hell, (who) unto those that ended up in the wrong neighborhood.

Let's reflect on Daniel briefly. Not technically a prophet himself, but a government official, Daniel described certain experiences of himself and his three friends in the first half of his book, always stressing how the Lord blessed them in critical situations. Then in the last half of the book, Daniel reproduced several visions that the Lord sent him. One of Daniel's major concerns was to explain the process of history. He was using insights gained from Jeremiah.

He placed Jewish history in the setting of the sequence of world empires and showed how the Lord was working out his will amidst the affairs of world history. Daniel wanted to encourage the exiled Jews to believe they still had a future in God's sovereign purposes. Christians are able to see these prophecies that this future is fulfilled in the coming of Christ.

Yes, now it is all about Jesus. The past is gone forever. We could consider many other names of people in the past. Still, the encouraging reflection was to sincerely emphasize the deep love, mercy, grace, and forgiveness that our loving heavenly Father possessed and was willing to give to those disobedient people then and even us now. Our God never changes. He showed love then, and he is still showing love and patience today. God desires that no one's spirit is lost after it exits the fleshly body and goes far away from his heavenly kingdom to the place called hell, where there are no cooling stations, a place of eternal torment day and night.

In Jesus, our good and awesome God has established the perfect process to save everyone. God sent his Son because of his love for us humans that everyone that was and will be born again in Jesus will be saved. The process is acknowledging and sincerely believing in Jesus Christ that he is the Son of God. We are repenting of the past sinful state of our life and asking our heavenly Father to forgive us through the shed blood of Jesus and asking Jesus to come into our hearts and spirits and be the ruler over our lives and refrain from going back to the past sinful actions of our lives. Through the process of water baptism, we are born again and will be able to grow now in righteousness with the help of the Holy Spirit.

If God desires to choose someone for his kingdom ministry, then blessed will that person be that understands and chooses to do God's will. There was once a man named Saul in the early days of Christianity, not long after Jesus had gone back to be with his Father in heaven. God chose this man, although this man was very passionate about chasing after these early Christians, putting them in jail for what they represented.

I do not have the correct reason why God chose him. All I know is that this man's life was completely turned around, and he became now the most talked-about Christian that worked very hard with the same passionate feeling that he had on the other side. He has helped and is still helping Christians stay on the narrow spiritual path through his writing to many churches and evangelizing, and even his name was changed.

By now, my genius readers have already figured out who this man was. Again, our reflections are inspired to demonstrate that whatever God desires will be done. If the heavenly Father explicitly calls you to his kingdom ministry, there is no need to try to run away like a man named Jonah did and was brought back in the belly of a whale. Absolutely amazing how even the big whale takes command from God, in that he went and positioned himself where God told him to be and waited for his passenger to be thrown overboard this boat and to snatch him before he would be drowned.

Let us get to this man named Saul by mentioning a Christian man named Stephen, chosen as one of seven by the people of the city in which they lived. These men were known to be of an honest report, full of Holy Ghost and wisdom. They were to handle the business of the early church to give Jesus's disciples more time to pray and concentrate on the ministry of the word.

So Stephen was anointed along with the others, and as the word of God and the church increased, Stephen was full of faith and power and did great wonders and miracles among the people. Certain high priests of the synagogue were not able to resist the wisdom and the Spirit of the way Stephen spake, so they conspired against him, saying they heard him speak blasphemous words against Moses and God, which of course he did not do.

And so they stirred up the elders, people, and the scribes and caught Stephen and brought him to their council. They set false witnesses against him and eventually decided to stone him to death, which they did. The witnesses laid their clothes at a young man's feet, whose name was Saul. A godly innocent man was being stoned to death, and through his faithfulness, even while they stoned him, Stephen still called upon God, saying, "Lord Jesus, receive my spirit." And he kneeled down and cried with a loud voice and said, "Lord, lay not this sin to their charge." And when he had said this, he fell asleep, or I could say that he died.

And now back to the man named Saul who had consented to Stephen's death. During this time, there was great persecution of the church in Jerusalem, and so they scattered throughout the regions of Judaea and Samaria, except for the apostle. So now this man, Saul, began making havoc on the church, entering into every house, hauling away men and women, and committing them to prison. Let us read together what this evil man Saul did. Acts 9:1–9 reads,

> AND SAUL, yet breathing out threatenings and slaughter against the disciples of the Lord, went unto the high priest, And desired of him letters to Damascus to the synagogues, that if he found any of this way, whether they were man or women, he might bring them bound unto Jerusalem.

> And as he journeyed, he came near Damascus: and suddenly there shined round about him a light from Heaven: And he fell to the earth, and heard a voice saying unto him, Saul, Saul, why persecutest thou me? And he said, Who art thou, Lord? And the Lord said, I am Jesus whom thou persecutest: it is hard for thee to kick against the pricks. And he trembling and astonished said, Lord, what wilt thou have me to do? And the Lord said unto him, arise, and go into the city, and it shall be told thee what thou must do.

> And the men which journeyed with him stood speechless, hearing a voice, but seeing no man. And Saul arose from the earth; and when his eyes were opened, he saw no man: but they led him by the hand, and brought him into Damascus. And he was three days without sight, and neither did eat nor drink.

That was a terrible experience and the calling to the ministry that this man Saul had. For the same people he was persecuting, God's power would have him join them with more zeal through his experience. Through the working of God's Spirit through other disciples, this Saul was brought before the disciples, who initially were skeptical because of the things he had been doing to Christians. However, he was now talking and functioning totally like a completely different person with sincerity. Saul is a very good example of God's amazing love, grace, and mercy.

The complete change in this man's life shows that God can clean up anyone in the name of Jesus and the working power of the Holy Spirit. We humans are in no position to give up on anyone or even throw the stone. The best thing for us to do, even if our loved ones or anyone we minister to shows resistance, is to pray for them and ask God to do his will in their lives in the name of Jesus, who is God the Son.

God the Son, Jesus, is so passionate about doing his Father's will, more than we can comprehend. Jesus will not do anything on his own unless his heavenly Father is in total agreement. So the Trinity of heaven desires to use this vessel with the name Saul, whose name will be eventually changed to Paul. And so through the ministry of a Christian man named Ananias, Jesus, through the Holy Spirit, sent him to this Saul, although he had a little reluctancy based on the knowledge of what he had heard and known about Saul. Please let us read this true event together that took place between four to seven years after Jesus's crucifixion in the year 30 AD. Acts 9:10–22 reads,

> And there was a certain disciple at Damascus, named Ananias; and to him said the Lord in a vision, Ananias. And he said, behold, I am here, Lord. And the Lord said unto him, Arise, and go into the street which is called Straight, and inquire in the house of Judas for one called Saul, of Tarsus: for, behold he prayeth, And hath seen in a vision a man named Ananias coming in, and putting his hand on him, that he might receive his sight. Then Ananias answered, Lord, I have heard by many of this man, how much evil he hath done to thy saints at Jerusalem: And here he hath authority from the chief priests to bind all that call on thy name.

> But the Lord said unto him, Go thy way: for he is a chosen vessel unto me, to bear my name before the Gentiles, and kings, and the children of Israel: For I will show him how great he must suffer for my name's sake. And Ananias went his way, and entered into the house; and putting his hands on him said, Brother Saul, the Lord even Jesus, that appeared

unto thee in the way as thou camest, hath sent me. that thou mightest receive thy sight, and be filled with the Holy Ghost. And immediately there fell from his eyes as it had been scales: and he received sight forthwith, and arose, and was baptized.

And when he had received meat, he was strenghtened. Then was Saul certain days with the disciples which were at Damascus. And straitway he preached Christ in the synagogues, that he is the Son of God. But all that heard him were amazed, and said; Is not this he that distroyed them which called on this named in Jerusalem, and came hither for that intent, that he might bring them bound unto the chief priest? But Saul increased the more in strength, and confounded the Jews which dwelt at Damascus, proving that this is very Christ.

My sisters and brothers in Christ, God can do all things through Christ Jesus. From the example of Saul's experiences and the work, he had to accomplish throughout his ministry. Through many struggles and tribulations, the evidence is clear that our heavenly Father can choose whom he desires to work in the kingdom-building ministry. We have to always remember that Christ's church is not in the hands of bishops who want to have their own airplanes and limousines, wearing three-piece suits, or pastors who cannot help themselves get in the way of the honor, praise, and glory going up to God. The Holy Spirit is in charge and will use you or me with God's approval.

Much later on the island of Cyprus for the first time, Saul was called Paul. We now know the apostle Paul, who wrote many letters to the churches with strong wording of encouragement and spiritual conduct of that the lives that are lived that any follower of Jesus Christ should have. With the intent of helping Christians then and even now stay on the narrow path that will lead to God's kingdom, God gave Saul a new heart, and his life was instantly changed to a brilliant minister of the word of God. He was well-educated and very eloquent in ministering then and now the righteousness of God.

We should not view our heavenly Father's and Creator's desires and will with a lightness of heart, whatever the Holy Spirit, who again is the administrator of the church, assigned in our hearts to be done. We need always to be passionate and real about our work in the kingdom ministry. Let us always continue to pray and ask God for spiritual increase because Jesus is soon to return to retrieve the righteous people of his church.

The separation of the sheep from the goats is very real. This is a warning for anyone playing church just to impress or deceive others like wolves in sheep's clothing. God knows all hearts and all the motives of why we do what we do, and no one knows the minute or the hour when Christ will come. Be ready for your spiritual transition and the direction in which your new body will go up or down. Hallelujah, Hallelujah to our heavenly Father's most Holy Name. Glory, honor, and praises be to him forever and ever. Amen.

10

Take a Closer Look at Faith

In this book, there is a lot of fascinating information that you are going to enjoy reading. Taking a closer look at faith has been chosen for this chapter for a couple of reasons. In chapter 1, we read about the awesomeness of the Creator. And there is a lot more to be said concerning our loving God. Faith in God is essential for a total appreciation of all the good news and educational reasoning ahead as you continue reading. Faith is born out of a strong belief. Hebrew 11: 6 reads, "But without faith, it is impossible to please him: for he that cometh to God must believe that he is and that he is a rewarder of them that diligently seek him."

Faith is primarily a chapter in this book because it is the strong foundation that everything else in our spiritual growing life is built on. A person has to honestly believe that there is a supreme, spiritual God, which is above all that exists, and he is the Creator of this vast universe and everything in it. The belief has to be in the heart that the Creator loves his human creation so much that he sent his only begotten Son to die on the cross so we as sinners could get a rebirth back to the spiritual connections he had intended for us (John 3:16).

A definition of faith means complete trust or confidence in someone or something. Faith is a strong belief in God, or the doctrines of a religion, based on spiritual apprehension rather than proof. Many people ask, "What is the true meaning of faith?" The answer: Faith means belief, firm persuasion in what we hope for, and the assurance that the Lord is working, even though we cannot see it. Faith also knows that no matter the situation, the Lord will work on it in our lives or someone else's. God blesses everyone who can believe and cultivate faith in their hearts. The level of how much belief there is causes faith not to be the same in everyone. Because of faith, our precious hope is born, and the hope we carry in our hearts will propel us as believers to higher spiritual heights. So when the enemy uses his cunning influences to distract us from getting us back down, we will boldly tell him, "Stand down, Satan, because we are not coming down." The enemy of God does not want to see any of us clinging on to faith and hope and growing spiritually strong.

So many questions are often asked, like, "What went wrong? Why is it so challenging for people to generate and maintain faith to be beneficial when needed?" Just about everyone, I believe, does have an understanding of what faith is all about. So another question is, "Did humans lose the ability to generate and maintain trust and faith as they should be? Does the lack of faith cultivation and development have anything to do with Adam and Eve falling from grace?"

The Bible is the master of godly information that we can run to as we seek answers to our questions, and the Bible says that we are all born in sin and shaped in iniquity. Is that what produces the lack of faith in many? So then, as you can see, there can be many questions. So let's look at a few situations. Read on, please. Your reading is going to be very interesting.

Let me share this understanding that the power of faith reflects the omnipotent nature of the almighty Creator, who bestowed trust on his own. Let us also remember that when God was communicating with Adam in the garden of Eden, it would seem then that faith was at its highest peak. Adam was full of faith and not doubtful in any way or form that God would not show up at the appointed time. They had a lot to talk about in this great beginning. Let us not forget that God told the man he made out of the dust of the ground to name all the creatures in the garden. A lot of communication was going on between them. Adam most likely explains to God why he gave the name he did to each of the creatures. We probably all would agree that Adam did a perfect job naming all he did. He was in a place of perfection, with nothing negative on his conscience.

It has been proven that a stained conscience can and does generate doubt in people. And at that time, the man, Adam, had not done anything wrong he was aware of, and so nothing was on his conscience that would interfere with maintaining the happiness he was feeling with his Creator. And since God bestowed faith on his own, Adam received his total share of it. I am sure that his faith then was much larger than a mustard seed, which is only 0.1 by 0.03 millimeters in size.

Jesus mentioned the mustard seed-size faith to Peter and four other disciples one day. They were all on a boat when they encountered a terrible storm. Jesus was taking a nap, and these guys thought they were going to die out there. Jesus woke up right on time, saw them panicking, and said to them, "Why are you afraid? Have you still no faith?" He most likely directed his comment to Peter since he was always the up-front guy. And, of course, the Bible tells us that Jesus calms the sea.

Jesus's primary focus was to generate faith that he saw was lacking in people throughout his life and ministry, even as he healed many. Why was Jesus so big on cultivating trust? Was it because he had an enormous amount of faith to be at one with his heavenly Father? As we do know, Jesus did not have an earthly father, as we all do. Then he would have been subjected to the same, born in sin and shaped in iniquity as we are. No, Jesus had a heavenly Father who was the Creator. In all of the miracles he performed to show the power of God, the main emphasis was on generating faith. And he permanently recognized those that possessed a little and commended them for the faith they had in him.

So let us reflect a little on the garden of Eden. Adam was doing very well. Although seeing a lot of the animals seem to be pairing up, that probably gave him a lonely feeling because feelings were already a part of him. Then the most beautiful of the many creatures he had ever seen and was more like him than all the others was standing before him. That was the best day of his existence. He probably thought, *God, you have outdone yourself.* All Adam knew was that he felt a little exhausted as if he were in a deeper sleep than he ever had before. Adam used to stay up late by himself getting his work done, but he had never felt this tired before, like something was taken from him. His heavenly Father did not keep him in the dark, but he technologically sent him information about his soon encounter, and there she was, a brand-new beauty he had to find a name for that would be fitting for her.

Adam sounded like he was a little tongue-tied or speaking out of uncontrolled excitement. Genesis 2:22–23 says, "And the rib, which the Lord God had taken from man, made he a woman, and brought her unto him. And Adam said, this is now bones of my bones, and flesh of my flesh: she shall be called Woman because she was taken out of man."

Maybe the nosy serpent was there and saw her too. This snake, who used to walk upright, was always jealous of the humans because they were so different from every other creature and spoke more intelligently than he did. And so he was vulnerable for Satan to use him for his madness until God cursed him to walk on his belly all his life (Genesis 3:14). Adam was overexcited about how his life was being turned around. If someone else were there to say, "Calm down, my brother. Take it easy. Do not get carried away," that would have helped him.

No, Adam did not need any input from anyone. The brother was lovestruck, love at first sight. Of all the creatures Adam was naming before that day, he never saw anyone with such beauty, which was so much more like him. That is why he was alone until then. That day Adam knew that God truly loved him, but there was an enemy that did not like anything he was seeing, pondering why God was so kind and friendly to these humans and the human was giving him all the praise. We know who that was. That was Satan, of course.

He wanted the praise the humans were given to the Creator, so he came up with a plan, thinking that since the serpent was on speaking terms with the humans and the snake was brilliant and very good with words, he was an excellent candidate to use to twist the command that God had given them. Genesis 3:1 said the serpent was subtle. Its malicious wisdom was high in contrast to Adam and Eve. The snake was brilliant. The dictionary version of a subtle person is cleverly using indirect methods to achieve something, crafty, cunning, and sly. That is why Satan chose to use him. Satan is still using people instead of a snake to carry on his ungodly work, even now in our generation. Everyone needs to be cautious of thoughts and ideas that present themselves because not everything sounds good, and God will keep us on that narrow path that Jesus said will lead to eternal life.

The cunning serpent, acting like he was the wise one, probably did not know that Satan was using him when he approached him with the idea of giving the beautiful lady an urgent message. Satan could have offered the snake a gift of some sort for his expertise way of communicating. Eve was approached charmingly, the serpent acting like a friend. Just like how friends are hurting friends even now.

He could have said, "Hello, Eve. Good morning, beautiful lady. It seems that you slept well last night because you look very energetic this morning. What did you do with your long hair? It is looking adorable. Are you still using that mango juice?"

He waited for her to respond because good conversation generates friendship, so be careful of sweet-talking people. Sometimes their intent is not good.

Then the serpent said, "Come to think about it, pretty lady, there is something significant that you will love to hear, good news."

Eve became curious and anxious to listen to this good news. "Tell me. Tell me quickly," she said. "I have to rush home to my husband."

The serpent promptly reflected her attention to a conversation about a fruit they had with God.

"This news is very impressive, Mr. Snake," she may have said. "How do you know all these things?"

"I have my source, good lady," the snake most likely replied.

The snake did not tell her that Satan, cast out of heaven, approached him to deliver the news to her. Satan always hides behind people, things, situations, and anything he can to avoid being blamed for the mess he often causes. That is why we have to call his name as Jesus did, speaking to Peter, said, "Get behind me, Satan," to let him know that we are conscious of him trying to deceive us.

She listened to him, and a seed was planted in her and began to grow very quickly. She had the freedom of choice. She chose to follow his instructions and gave the same idea to her husband, who loved her very much, and now for Adam and Eve, the time of disobedience arrived because of the freedom of choice. Most often, people still make the wrong choices in their lives. Everything that Adam and Eve did were induced to all the generations after in our genes. The blame game began after God questioned them about what they had done. Adam blamed it on the woman; the woman blamed the serpent. People still push the blame around now every chance they get to do so.

The sentencing came on them because of disobedience, doing what was wrong. God put Adam and Eve out of the beautiful garden. Did they leave certain human beneficial characteristic qualities in the garden, like faith and other qualities that would have given humans too much power outside the gate of power? The garden was a place of enormous strength with regular visitation from the Creator. It is very challenging for us to easily comprehend the disappointment and loss that Adam felt now, realizing that so much is directly changing in his life. From paradise lost to paradise regained is what Jesus now represents. He is currently the new Adam for Christians worldwide who believe in the Genesis Bible story.

Children were born to Adam and Eve after they left the garden of Eden, and so all humans and their descendants are born with a sinful nature. No one has to teach a child how to do wrong. It seems that doing wrong is automatic. We teach our children to do what is right in the best we can. Conscience now is the ruler of the day. Please read the Adam and Eve story in Genesis 3:1–20. There, you will become aware that immediately after they ate the fruit they were told not to eat and heard God's voice, the couple hid and took leaves for clothing because negative thinking now began. Clothing was not the main factor they thought about before.

Believing that someone will do for you when in your heart you know you have done them wrong is not easy to do. Our conscience is interfering with the growth of our faith in a significant way. Sin nature is still in us. Even if we did not do wrong, we still have the stained conscience through inheritance from Adam and Eve. Conscience automatically generates doubt in all of us. People are having a problem with the generation and growth of faith. Could it be one reason why Jesus told the young man, Nicodemus, that he had to be born again for him to inherit the kingdom of God? Of course, not from his mother's womb, but a spiritual rebirth through water baptism to strip away that sin conscience that we all were born with and create a newness in us.

Jesus now, being the new Adam, wants so much for us to communicate with God again like Adam used to do before making the wrong decision. Faith is the foundation on which to build this new spiritual relationship with our Creator. The born-again process has to be genuine, sincere, and honest from the heart. Through this miraculous rebirth, humans can escape the bondage of the stained conscience and then will be able to communicate again with our heavenly Father with freedom of Spirit in the name of his Son, Jesus the Christ.

In churches worldwide, pastors call for their people to come to the altar and bring their burdens, situations, and concerns and leave them there through faith that our heavenly Father will take care of these things as only he can. People go up to the altar but bring back what they took up there back to their seats and back home with them. There is still a significant problem for people to put and leave things in the hands of God. Faith will cause someone else to misinterpret your action and think you do not care about a situation when others fall apart. Genuine faith generates boldness; it will cause you to push your way through many murky and troubled mountain-type situations that you first think you cannot climb.

Since this chapter is about faith, it is good that we reflect on the Bible story about the gentlewoman who had a medical blood problem that no one could cure for her. She spent everything she had and more, even borrowing from family and friends. The lady had to pay many doctors over the years of her turmoil. She may have even gone to see the voodoo person, and no one was able to cure her. Then one day she heard about this man who they said had turned water into wine, healed the sick, and gave another his sight back, but was many miles away from where she lived.

This information was like a seed planted in her, something she did not have before. She now believed someone would cure her. And so the lady began her journey to see the man they called Jesus. Her strong belief, the cornerstone of faith, kept her determination very strong to keep moving toward her goal. She finally made it and was able to press through the crowd, and as she touched the hem of his garment, Jesus recognized a certain feeling because of her faith, and Jesus healed her. When Jesus mentions mustard seed in Matthew 17:20, we need to understand that seeds are a process that allows growth from small to large. And just as a child grows to become bigger and stronger, so can our faith grow in our Creator, believing with confidence and a firm conviction that there is nothing impossible for God to do.

Life journey crosses many bridges and goes over many mountains, through valleys and plains. At times, you can feel like you are by the rivers of waters that David spoke about in the book of Psalm. Other times, you can feel like you are between a rock and a hard place, and still, at different times, you can feel like you are in the desert all alone. No, in all of these situations mentioned and more, have faith, sisters and brothers. God will be there with you and help you make it in any circumstances if you only put your sincere trust in him. Take another look at faith. The Bible said that faith comes by hearing the words of God. Listen to what other people receive because of their faith. God is not partial; your Creator will do the same for you.

It is not our flesh that does great works of power. The Spirit of God does the job in our situation. Our flesh is only a container of an enormous spirit in us that makes the connection with God's Holy Spirit. Understanding what Adam lost the most in his situation was the spiritual connection and the good relationship he had with God. It was not all about the flesh. Only through the new rebirth through Jesus, our Savior, can we get back what was lost and assume our rightful position with faith. A man asked the disciple of Jesus if he could buy some of the power they had, and the answer was no. Each person has to make up their mind to choose the narrow road that leads to the kingdom of God. On that road, faith will journey beside you.

Would you please reflect on a few of the many people that faith moves them to please God? Hebrew 11:4–10 states,

> By faith Abel offered unto God a more excellent sacrifice than Cain, by which he obtained witness that he was righteous, God testifying of his gifts: and by it he being dead yet speaketh. By faith Enoch

was translated that he should not see death; and was not found, because God had translated him: for before his translation he had this testimony, that he pleased God. By faith Noah, being warned of God of things not seen as yet, move with fear, prepared an ark to the saving of his house; by the which he condemned the world, and become heir of the righteousness which is faith. By faith Abraham, when he was called to go out into a place which he should after receive for an inheritance, obeyed; and he went out, not knowing whither he went. By faith he sojourned in the land of promise, as in a strange country, dwelling in tabernacles with Isaac and Jacob, the heirs with him of the same promise: For he looked for a city which hath foundations whose builder and maker is God.

Verse 17 reads, "By faith Abraham, when he was tried, offered up Isaac: and he that had received the promises offered up his only begotten son."

These examples of people of faith written in the New Testament serve as a reflection on these long-ago generations that believed and had faith just like us. Jesus knew about faith long before he came to earth from heaven, and he works very hard to help those people who saw him then and for every generation since then to understand that without faith, it is impossible to connect with and please God. All the healing he did was to demonstrate the tremendous spiritual power of God and plant the seed of faith. When we minister to the unsaved, we have to stress and implant the understanding that the first thing that has to develop in their hearts is to believe based on us sharing the words of God, which is the good soil that will allow faith to grow. As Christians, we have no choice but to believe and have faith that Jesus went to prepare a place for us and that he will come back and get all of us to enjoy that promise with him.

Why do all Christians not possess the same level of faith? Is it that it is not thought about as much as it should in the mind of all Christians? We have to be very careful not to judge. Instead pray that the Holy Spirit in his work continuation will impress upon the hearts of all God's people that faith is not just the order of the day because it is the driving force that keeps our precious hope alive. As Christians, we always need to remember that the enemy, who is a liar, will try to let so many other things of the world seem to be more important than what we need to be the focus as we journey to the promised place of God, which is not New York City. The enemy is also bringing a lot of persecution on many Christians in different parts of the world, and many prayers are needed for them. Many people take their freedom of worship for granted, as some do other blessings as well. God's enemy, Satan, still does have a lot of influences here on Earth, but be reminded that Jesus said, "And I say also unto thee, That thou art Peter, and upon this rock I will build my church; and the gates of hell shall not prevail against it" (Matthew 16:18).

The church is Jesus's follower and not the building we jump around in. It does not matter if the building is prominent, medium, or minor, for it is not the size of the building that opens the gate of heaven for us. And we are not a better Christian because we worship in a megachurch and look down on the worshipers pouring their hearts out to the Lord in a small church on the corner. Whether in the jungle or a big city, every Christian worldwide is striving for the same everlasting life with Jesus. Keep the faith, brothers and sisters, no matter what the situation. Hold on tight as you can. We cannot let anything separate us from the love of God through Jesus our Lord. Also remember that we cannot keep ourselves. The Holy Spirit of God, connecting with our inner spirit, allows us to survive the tyranny of the evil one.

Now faith is the substance of things hoped for, the evidence of things not seen. For by it the elders obtained a good report. Through faith we understand that the worlds were framed by the word of God, so that things which are seen were not made of things which do appear. (Hebrews 11:1–3)

11

Spiritual Increase from Our Creator

The word *increase* carries specific meanings: to become more significant in quantity, to grow and augment (as plants), to advance in numbers or values, and to increase in knowledge, which also comes with age. Our heavenly Father designs humans with the ability to increase as we grow in various ways—in strength, knowledge, height, closeness to him, love, and happiness as we travel—through the winding road of life.

Of all the increases that will be experienced in our lifetime, there is one that is more important than all the others, spiritual increase. The Bible says that God is a Spirit, and those that worship him must worship him in spirit and truth. It is not how big the church is that we go to, how well-dressed the pastor is on Sunday morning, how many new and nice cars are in the parking lot of the church, or how much noise is between the four walls that impress or invite God to pay attention to the worship service. The heart and lifestyle of each person in that building have to be spiritually connected with God's Holy Spirit to generate true worship to God.

The spiritual increase from totally committing ourselves will allow us to grow stronger and closer to our loving heavenly Father. Our inner spirit connects more with the Holy Spirit of God. In these very turbulent and troublesome times that we live in, prayer for a spiritual increase to withstand God's enemy's cunning and vicious attitude should be at the forefront of our daily lives. God's enemy, the one called Satan, is spoken of in the Bible as going about like a roaring lion and even more so like a starving lion devouring all he can is real. Without the Holy Spirit's help, who is always connected with our spirit as children of God, life situations and concerns can be overwhelming. We can get distracted from the godly focus that is needed. This spiritual struggle and giving up along the way is happening to many people that love the Lord.

Let us reflect on a human like us who believes and knows that he needed help real quickly from God through a specific increase. This man was a young king who needed a considerable boost for the responsibility he saw before him. The young king was King Soloman, the son of King David, who rules over Israel for forty years, seven years in Hebron and thirty-three years in Jerusalem (1 Kings 2:11). Let us read together about this from the word of God. 2 Chronicles 1:6–12 says,

> And Solomon went up thither to the brasen altar before the Lord, which was at the tabernacle of the congregation, and offered a thousand burnt offerings upon it. In that night did God appear unto Solomon, and said unto him, Ask what I shall give thee. And Solomon said unto GOD, thou hast shewed great mercy unto my father, and hast made me to reign in his stead. Now, O Lord God, let thy promise unto David my father be established: for

thou hast made me King over a people like the dust of the Earth in multitude.

Give me now wisdom and knowledge, that I may go out and come in before this people: for who can judge this thy people, that is so great? And God said to Solomon, Because this was in thine heart, and thou hast not asked riches, wealth, or honor, nor the life of thine enemies, neither yet hast long life; but hast asked wisdom and knowledge for thyself, that thou mayest judge my people, over whom I have made thee King: Wisdom and knowledge is granted unto thee; and I will give thee riches, and wealth, and honour, such as none of the kings have that had that have been before thee, neither shall there any after thee have the like. Then Solomon came from his journey to the high place that was at Gibeon to Jerusalem, from before the tabernacle of the congregation, and reigned over Israel.

There is only one Creator, God, and the heavenly host we can call on when we need help in things that we cannot wrap our arms around. Our loving heavenly Father created the vast universe, the heaven, the earth, and all the galaxies and planets, known and the many unknown. The Creator is the same God that provided the beautiful garden for the first man. And he also provided him with the first beautiful queen. He is the same God that gave Noah all the measurements, heights, and width to build an ark so they would survive the pending flood. That flood did come and transferred the condition of humanity, along with the family of eight with two kinds of every creature, from one dark age to another sunshine existence. That family of eight received from God a vast amount of increase in health, determination, wisdom, knowledge, and understanding to complete such a large project on time. They could not have completed these tasks without the various increases from their God and helper.

Our loving God is not partial like the various partiality we often see or experience in selfish people. God will bless us with increase as he gave them. We just probably need to communicate with him more often. We all need growth from time to time as we travel through the many storms of our lives. The Creator is the same then, now, and forever will be. The precious seeds of confidence and faith in our loving God that do not have to sleep or slumber are precious commodities that we must ask him to sow in us as newborn spiritual children. And as we grow spiritually, we will understand more and more the importance of maximizing our prayer life with God. Communication with God has to be a constant daily way of life to stay focused on walking through the valley of the shadow of death and not to fear any evil.

It is comforting to know that God is by your side when you wake up in the morning, when you say "goodbye" and "have a nice day" to your loved ones, or when you say "I am gone now," you know that the Holy Spirit of God is going with you. We might even have angels as spiritual bodyguards keeping unseen enemies from blocking our path because we should never forget that there is a spiritual world coexisting with the physical world of airplanes, trucks, buses, and buildings. The Bible said that humans are made a little lower than angels. I believe that as spiritual beings, they are more advanced than we will ever be. They have much more intellect and know and understand the universe's operation more than the extraordinary scientists and the great astronomers.

As humans, we should give the Creator daily thanks for blessing us to have dominion over the creatures of the earth. There is so much knowledge here on this earth to partake of and to continuously increase in wisdom, knowledge, and understanding. So many people never grow to their full potential to be all they can be. Circumstances, environments, the unfortunate lack of a good education, family history, and childhood growth are just some of the many reasons for the disparity, no matter what the circumstances are, as long as a person is breathing. They have a mind that with the help of God and the determination on their part, something can come out of nothing. Many people cry about what they do not have and do not exercise the effort to put themselves in the way for a better outcome to happen.

Many people have testimonies of where their life was and where it is now. People have said how they were homeless, starving, or broke or even came back from incarceration, and with effort and God's blessings, they sometimes cannot believe how their lives have changed for the better. And then some had many opportunities and did not take advantage of them. Others do not seem to even want to try doing better. It's so hard sometimes to witness some people that function in a way as to let learning pass them by. They show no sign of wanting to increase. Some people do not believe that God can and will help them if they only try. The Bible said that faith without work is dead. First, you have to have faith that the same God that allows the person to accumulate a mansion will help you in your endeavor to get an apartment, and then you have to put forth the effort. Then the blessings of God will take you to a moon-type existence.

Let's consider the condition that God had placed Adam and Eve to live in the garden of Eden, with everything they needed at the time to live and eat very well. It should give all of us the assurance that God desires us to live a good, decent, and prosperous life here on this earth now. How blessed we are in these times to have so many technologies functioning all around us. If you want to bake a special cake, Grandma in the UK does not have to be disturbed. You go to your phone, and YouTube will take you through step by step. And consider how wonderful it is to go on Zoom and speak to Aunt Lisa in Africa, Cousin Darlene in Pennsylvania, Uncle Peter in Florida, and Aunt Doris in Canada at the same time for planning the family reunion next year. There are so many increases in blessings, even in technology all around us.

Give God the glory every day of your life. Recognize from whom all our blessings flow. Give your Creator thanks that you are breathing right now on this side of the grass and continue to do your very best to enjoy your given piece of the life pie. People are flowing at different altitudes in the movement of life. Don't spend any time being jealous of anyone or looking down on another. Thank God for those ahead because they are just clearing the way for you to come from behind, and encourage those who may be dragging behind you because you are clearing the way for them. Just as God blesses those ahead, he will bless you and the others holding the rear.

Do the very best always with whatever you are blessed to have. Jesus had spoken in a parable in Matthew 25:14–30. Please let us read this together.

> For the Kindom of Heaven is as a man traveling into a far country, who called his own servants and delivered unto them his goods. And unto one he gave five talents, to another two and to another one; to every man according to his several ability; and straightway took his journey. Then he that had received the five talents went and traded with the same, and made them other five talents. And likewise he that had received two, he also gained other two. But he that had received one went and digged in the Earth, and hid his Lord's money.
>
> After a long time the Lord of those servants cometh, and reconeth with them. And so he that had received five talents came and brought other five talents, saying Lord, thou deliveredst unto me five talents: behold. I have gained beside them five talents more. His Lord said unto him, well done, thou good and faithful servant: thou hast been faithful over a few things, I will make thee ruler over many things:

enter thou into the joy of thy Lord. He also that had received two talents came and said, Lord, thou deliveredst unto me two talents: behold, I have gained two other talents beside them. His Lord said unto him, well done, good and faithful servant; thou hast been faithful over a few things, I will make thee ruler over many things: enter thou into the joy of thy Lord.

Then he which had received the one talent came and said, Lord, I knew thee that thou art an hard man, reaping where thou hast not sown, and gathering where thou hast not strawed: And I was afraid, and went and hid thy talent in the Earth: lo, there thou hast that is thine. His Lord answered and said unto him, Thou wicked and slothful servant, thou knewest that I reap where I sow not, and gather where I have not strawed: Thou oughtest therefore to have put my money to the exchangers, and then at my coming I should have received mine own with usury. Take therefore the talent from him, and give it unto him which hath ten talents. For unto every one that hath shall be given, and he shall have abundance: but from him that hath not shall be taken away even that which he hath. And cast ye the unprofitable servant into outer darkness: there shall be weeping and gnashing of teeth.

God gave all humans different gifts and abilities, and it is terrific when your blessings can be so filled to the brim and overflow unto being a blessing to others. Do not hide from yourself because you cannot. No one person knows or can do everything. That is why we all need each other, learning from some and encouraging others. It is said that it takes a village to raise a child. Time is the master of all because what goes around does come back around again. And remember, if you sow good seeds, a very good product of rewards will be reaped in time, and if you plant the terrible seed of discord in time, you will also reap an unhappy and uncomfortable result. And if it is all possible, live good and well with all the people you can. No person will be able to please everybody on this planet. That is why there has to be more than a one-party system.

So often we have heard what has been saying for a long time that God does not bless any mess. If spiritual increases are the desires of a person's heart, humility is one of the foundation pillars. The more spiritually stronger you grow, the more humble you will find yourself getting to be. And then one has to be so careful because so many people will take your meekness for weakness, and because you are humble, the belief you are soft with no backbone is not valid. Thank God that he knows what is in everyone's heart, and that should be the primary concern as we grow in God. The great King David said that God would spread a table before us in the presence of our enemy, and God will anoint our head with oil that our cup will be running over. And please do not forget that goodness and mercy shall follow you all the days of your life as you also recognize the presence of God in your life.

The countenance of the people of God should always be more uplifted than the people of the world. Even though we still have to deal with human issues and still have to pay Ceaser what belongs to Ceaser and the many bills that never seem to stop coming to live a comfortable life. Because we are children of the Most High God, we placed our burden on the shoulder of God because we are still living in a sinful physical world. Children of God are obedient and love the Lord more than the others that do not choose to live an obedient life before the Creator. We have to share the good news of God's kingdom as often as we can because God does not which for anyone to perish. Spiritual increases are needed for us to be as bold as we need to be to accomplish the work that is before us. Our loving

God will not allow more to come over you that you cannot generate the strength to stand firm and get the job done.

As you know, our God is the master of all technologies. We periodically input a form of technology in the reading to shed more understanding of the subject matter. And as we now are reasoning about the spiritual increase and how substantial it is, let us consider a very sophisticated component here on earth that is working for us, a transistor. It gives an increase in its own way. All electronics systems depend on the transistor for its ability to provide an increase in putting out more than it takes in. Amplification is a process to turn a small signal into a more significant signal. The transistor is in all electronic equipment, especially those that used speakers for the audio sound to be heard by others.

An example of the operation of the transistor in your radio or TV set is as follows. We previously spoke about transmitting and receiving signals from one phone to another or from the radio or TV station to your television or stereo system. There is an amplification process of the information sent over the airwave at the point of transmission and at the point of receiving what was sent. For instance, when the DJ speaks on the microphone or the music is being played, those audio signals are boosted up or amplified and made stronger to travel through the air space. But the signal gets weaker than when it left because of the distance. And so when it gets to the television, radio, or telephone, it is not strong enough to be heard by anyone through the speakers. So unseen by the eyes, many components inside the receiving equipment go to work, increasing these weak signals to allow us to hear what is sent.

Every electronic operation has an input, where the information is coming into the equipment. And the output of that put out that information after being processed and made more extensive. The transistor has its input and output. There are three contact points on the transistor: the emitter, the base, and the collector. It required a certain amount of DC voltage connected to it for it to operate. The information is an AC signal fed to the base, which is the input of the transistor, and the increase takes place and goes out by way of the collector, which is the output point of the transistor. The emitter controls the negative side of the operating voltage the transistor needs. A transistor can be connected for the input and output to be at different points.

Transistor increases can be continually increased, more and more, by connecting them in a series way, the output of the first one to the input of the second, the output of the second to the input of the third, the output of the third one to the input of the fourth, and so on. These transistors are considered to be connected in series, meaning one after the other. And then there is the larger and more powerful transistor connected directly to the speaker through a capacitor filter called the power transistor. It put so much out that it has to be provided a heat sink or something to keep it cool or from getting overheated.

I refer to these things that we see every day to give a broader understanding of the subject matter of increase. Now we also have what is referred to as a chip containing hundreds or even thousands of transistors that causes computers to operate at such fast speed. Often, the average consumer is only looking at the outside of the equipment, like the television. Still, there is a substantial, invisible-to-the-eyes movement of electrons on the inside of the television, in a world of its own doing what it does. So remember that a transistor is a three-terminal, solid-state semiconductor component that is used to increase and control the flow of electricity in a circuit. The ability of a transistor to magnify current is called amplification.

The spiritual world of God is not visible to our eyes, and the spiritual increase we get can be seen only from the conduct and action of an individual. Electricity is also an invisible, spiritual world given to us by God that the human's eyes cannot see. We cannot see it, but we know the work it does. It is not something to be played with even if you are trained to work with it. We cannot see God or the heavenly host; no one will see the Creator God and live. People saw Jesus when he was in the flesh but cannot see Jesus now back in the spirit world. We cannot see the angels or even the Holy Spirit that Jesus sent to us on the day of Pentecost to be our comforter and to guide and protect us, but we see all their handiworks and know they are there. To God the Creator be all the glory forever. If the awesome works of God are felt in your spirit as you read, then it is ok to say amen.

With the blessings of our loving heavenly Father's help, a spiritual magnification also takes place in humans. If and when anyone puts forth just a little effort to get right with God, the Holy Spirit is here and always ready to help to magnify or increase that earnest effort. It is as we are told that if we just open the door of our hearts, the Holy Spirit will come in. And when God the Holy Spirit comes into our hearts, it is also God the Father and God the Son because they are three-in-one. And again, when they come in, an instant automatic increase began right away. God will work with any human being who is ready to give their hearts to him because he loves us all, and he is the excellent loving source of ultimate spiritual power that every child of God needs.

The Creator in heaven can also send a signal to increase our health and help our infirmity or sickness, which we would call a miracle. Ponder or think about this Bible story example of a rich man coming to see Jesus and telling him that he left one of his servants back in his home very sick. And because of all the news he had heard about Jesus and being a very knowledgeable ruler, he knew that this man Jesus was not like the others that came into towns and cities, stayed at big hotels, and took people's money with promises never kept. This ruler believed, in his heart, that Jesus could heal his servant from right where he was and did not need to come to his house. And, of course, Jesus knew what was already in his heart because we cannot deceive God.

Jesus sent a signal straight to the sick man's body and rebooted it like we reboot a frozen computer right back to normal. Those people in the house were so astonished because they could not understand how such a rapid recovery took place as sick as the man was. They did not really know what had taken place until the ruler came back home, saw for himself the incredible technological power of God, and explained to them that he had gone to see the man called Jesus. These types of sending-signals technology to get things done in a distant place are what our loving God allows humans to learn, technology that God had been using before he even created our beautiful earth.

That is why these intelligent people in our modern technology superstorm can send lots of signals in space as they are doing to accomplish the many excellent space explorations—and communicating with people on the space station—flying helicopters on the Planet Mars, which is about 33.9 million miles from Earth (54.6 million kilometers). The distance in signal-sending is increasing rapidly by scientists, but our Creator can send a signal from heaven to his children here on earth faster than you can blink your eye. Scientists on Earth have to use the connection from one satellite to another to cover the vast distance, but God's signal comes straight to us from him. Spiritual increase in growing strong is available to everyone that calls on the name of Jesus and is ready and willing to allow him to rule their lives.

We, the people of God, can do all things through Christ Jesus, our Lord and Savior. Every one of us needs to increase in different ways. Everybody is not good at everything 100 percent. We all are born here on earth in sin and have various weaknesses of the flesh. But we have been born again as new creatures before God through the shed blood of Jesus who went to the cross for all of us. And now we must rely on him for all our new life sustenance through his Holy Spirit. We can always call on the name of Jesus, or God the Father, for help in time of need. We should all practice a daily routine in finding a time to communicate with our loving heavenly Father. This is what God desires for us to do, although he gives us freedom of choice and does not treat us like robots. God's grace and mercies will always follow us day by day.

We can use spiritual increase for all the many gifts God allows us to have. We can do better at everything we do for the glory of God. A preacher will preach better, a singer will sing better, a teacher will teach better, and even the musician will play better that even the person who use to find it hard to move in the pew will begin to dance for the Lord. The whole church will be on a higher spiritual level because of the vast increase. Each person will feel better within themselves, more now than before, enough to tell the enemy to step aside because the Spirit is now ruling over the urges of the fleshly lust. Thank you, heavenly Father, that we can call on you in the name of Jesus for the spiritual increase that comes from you and only you, oh God.

12

Angels Are Watching Over Me

Let us begin this chapter with a clear understanding of all it means when a human being submits and gives all of their heart to the heavenly host. Everyone who gives their heart to God gets treated the same way in the past, present, and future. So the same commitment God gave to godly men and woman in times past continue forever. Let us look at Isaiah 41:10. "Fear thou not; for I am with thee: be not dismayed; for I am thy God: I will strengthen thee: yea, I will help thee: yea, I will uphold thee with the right hand of my righteousness." That was our Creator and God speaking.

Now let us hear from his only begotten Son, Jesus, in Matthew 28:18–20.

And Jesus came and spake unto them, saying, All power is given unto me in Heaven and in Earth. Go ye therefore, and teach all nations, baptizing

> them in the name of the Father, and of the Son,
> and of the Holy Ghost: Teaching them to observe
> all things whatsoever I have commanded you: and,
> lo, I am with you always, even unto the end of the
> world. Amen.

God the Father, God the Son, and God the Holy Spirit are three-in-one. Wherever there is one, all three almighty powers are there, so the angels are on standby to do what thus saith the Lord. That is why we can be confident that if we are doing our part by ignoring the fleshly desires, walking, and serving God in Spirit and truth, we can let Romans 8:31 be our pillar that we rest our heads on. "What shall we then say to these things? If God be for us, who can be against us?"

Many people have not grasped the powers that surround the children of God. Thank God for Jesus. All powers are in Jesus's hands forever and ever. When anyone joins the army of the Lord, not just angels are watching, but the heavenly host.

King David said, "the Lord is my shepherd," and this statement can be applied to anyone who is in the army of the Lord. So can the statement that angels are watching over me. It can also be spoken by anyone in the army of the Lord. We know that God, the Creator of everything that exists in heaven and on earth, is real. We know that Jesus is alive and by his heavenly Father's side. And from all the evidence the disciples had seen, we know that the Holy Spirit came to us as Jesus had promised on the day of Pentecost. We also know that angels are mentioned in the Bible a total of 295 times, 108 times in the Old Testament and 187 times in the New Testament. The evidence is clear that angels are real, they do exist, and they are doing fantastic work for the Creator. And it is on the Bible evidence that I rest my case to all those who might have doubt in the existence and functioning of angels.

The Bible lets us understand that humans are made a little lower than angels. So they are far more intelligent than humans are. So consider how sophisticated and intelligent many humans are, with the intellect to create all the beautiful homes we live in and the many things we enjoy, like bridges, tunnels, planes, trains, electronic technology, unique medical technology, and all the other many things that keep us sane and have us living in close to a paradise condition. If humans can do as much as they are doing, then think of all the marvelous things angels can and are doing in the service of the Creator in this vast universe. Angels have the ability and capability to materialize themselves into humans form and at one time were being used as messengers to humans

We know that God the Creator created heaven and all the heavenly hosts before the earth. And so, angels must have looked on to witness the marvelous creation of humans. For the rest of our days on this earth, let us give thanks to our heavenly Father for everything that our brain and senses can comprehend and even for the many things we do not yet understand. Still, we know that everything that God did exists for our good and survival on this tiny speck of the Milky Way galaxy. We should all be very proud of Daniel speaking boldly to the king in Daniel 6:22. "My God hath sent his angel, and hath shut the lions' mouths, that they have not hurt me: forasmuch as before him innocency was found in me; and also before thee. O King, have I done no hurt." That king had shown no respect for the almighty Creator who could have zapped him as people do to a fly. We have heard of the true story about Daniel being thrown into the lion's den.

So the king came back to the lion's den the following morning after a sleepless night of rage, expecting to see Daniel no more because he had ordered his guards to throw Daniel in and seal the lion's cage for them to have a nice human feast. But to his surprise, as we read from Daniel 6:20, "And when he came to the den, he cried with a lamentable voice unto Daniel: and the king spake and said to Daniel, O Daniel, servant of the living God, is thy God, whom thou servest continually, able to deliver thee from the lions?"

Daniel still was so full of humility that he did not even curse at the king or show him his right-hand fingers what number he is in his book, as some people of today would.

Me, myself, and I do not need a bodyguard because I know for sure that angels are watching over me and have kept me from much harm or even death, but it was not my time as yet to transition to the other side. I have heard many people give their testimonies over the years of how they were saved from being hurt and could not understand why they were not. All they knew is that it must be God that had saved them.

God is not partial. What he has done for Daniel and many others throughout the many generations, he will also do for you and me. I have a true testimony story of Mr. G as a young boy. One day he was on his way to the post office to retrieve a package sent for him and two of his sisters, Sylvia and Joan. It was quite a long walk for the young man in the heat of that day, and so he got very excited when he saw a truck backed up to a loading dock with no activity because the driver seemed to be doing his paperwork.

Mr. G hopped onto the back of the parked truck with his two feet hanging down with the vehicle's tail end about twelve inches from touching the concrete dock. As he sat there waiting to be escorted away toward his destination, someone said to him, "Get down now. Instead of the truck going forward, it could back up and touch the concrete wall." He noted that the urging was so strong that he immediately jumped off the truck, and just as he moved away, to his surprise, the truck backed up and hit the concrete very hard. The impact would have broken his two feet to pieces. Mr. G said his guardian angel saved him that day to allow him to dance in church, and he considers himself still blessed to having his two feet intact.

I have another testimony from Sister Gordon. One day as she was standing at her window looking outside and watching the kids at play, suddenly someone said, "Move away from the window." She did right away. Just then, a bullet came busting through the glass window exactly where she was standing. The bullet would have gone right through her if it were not for her guardian angel.

Many people genuinely believe that their guardian angel saves their lives or keeps them from serious harm. An angel is a brilliant and very intelligent, morally good spiritual being created by God. We know from the word of God that there are archangels, angels with high ranks. There are seven names of archangels known to us thus far: Michael, Gabriel, Uriel, Raphael, Selaphiel, Raquel, and Jegudiel. We also know that Satan was a very highly decorated angel who lost his way and was cast out of heaven along with those other angels, of which he had a strong influence over them.

Many angels are doing various works in the universe and also working in and around the earth. Although they are above us and could use us like robots, they cannot go against the will of God, so there are things they could prevent but cannot do so. They will not prevent a person from exercising their God-given free will unless the Creator instructs them to do so. This means they will not keep you from sinning if you choose to do so. And when a person's time on this earth has come to an end and they have to transition to the other side, your guardian angel will escort you but will not stop the process. An angel was the one who materialized into human form and gave the good news to Abraham that his wife, Sarah, was going to have a son. Sarah overheard the conversation, not knowing who the guy was, and probably thought that her dear husband and his friend were smoking the wrong stuff again.

God-loving and caring angels keep up with the functioning of humans. They want to see us do well before their Creator. They are proud of us when we give ourselves to God and live an extraordinary godly life. Jesus said in Luke 15:10, "Likewise, I say unto you, there is joy in the presence of the angels of God over one sinner that repenteth."

Many people are not conscious of how well-loved we are by the heavenly host. These same angels never die because only flesh dies; spirits do not. They saw our loving Creator permitted his only begotten Son to come down to earth from his throne, take on the human form through birth, and then sacrifice that flesh for the redemption of us all. So they see that we are very special to their Creator and will do anything they can to guide and protect us from harm and dangers. The angels will do so to honor God.

After the prominent temptation of Jesus, Satan lost because Jesus did not do anything that Satan had suggested, in view of all the given tactics he uses. The Bible tells us in Matthew 4:11, "Then the devil leaveth him, and, behold, angels came and ministered unto him."

Remember, when you are being enticed into doing something wrong by the enemy, please know that your angel is there but cannot intervene forcefully to take away your rights of free will. God always, through his angels, gives us a way out of severe temptation, but frequently the enemy's voice is booming and causes us not to hear the quiet voice trying to save us. The satisfaction of the flesh is so intense. It is like, whatever the flesh wants, the flesh gets. And so we all, through the power of God's Holy Spirit and the encouragement of our guardian angel, have to keep this flesh of ours under subjection and study the words of God and read inspired books, as you are doing now to show ourselves approved. Some temptation urges are so strong that you have to call on Jesus quickly if you are not like those who put their Bible on the shelf when they want to do their own thing.

If you had never thought before how protected you can be by standing up for your God and being protected by God's holy angels, please let me share this story to make you a believer in angels. You don't even have to get your Bible. It is quoted in your hand to read now. Daniel 3:8–30 reads,

> Wherefore at that time certain Chaldeans came near, and accused the Jews. They spake and said to the King Nebuchadnezzar, O King, live for ever. Thou, O King, hast made a decree, that

every man that shall hear the sound of the cornet, flute, harp, sackbut, psaltery, and dulcimer, and all kind of musick, shall fall down and worship the golden image: And whoso falleth not down and worshippeth, that he should be cast into the midst of a burning fiery furnace.

There are certain Jews whom thou hast set over the affairs of the province of Babylon, Shadrach, Meshach. and Abednego; these men, O King, have not regarded thee: they serve not thy gods, nor worship the golden image which thou hast set up. Then Nebuchadnezzar in his rage and fury commanded to bring Shadrach, Meshach, and Abed-nego. Then they brought these men before the King. Nebuchadnezzar spake and said unto them, Is it true, O Shadrach, Meshach, and Abed-nego, do not ye serve my gods, nor worship the golden image which I have set up?

Now if ye be ready that at what time ye hear the sound of the cornet, flute, harp, sacbut, psaltery, and dulcimer, and all kinds of musick, ye fall down and worship the image which I have made; well: but if ye worship not, ye shall be cast the same hour into the midst of a burning fiery furnace; and who is that God that shall deliver you out of my hands? Shadrach, Meshach, and Abed-nego, answered and said to the King, O Nebuchadnezzar, we are not careful to answer thee in this matter. If it be so, our God whom we serve is able to deliver us from the burning fiery furnace, and he will deliver us out of thine hand, O King. but if not, be it known unto thee, O King, that we will not serve thy gods, nor worship the golden image which thou hast set uo.

Then was Nebuchadnezzar full of fury, and the form of his visage was changed against Shadrach, Meshach, and Abed-nego: therefore he spake, and commanded that they should heat the furnace one seven times more that it was wont to be heated. And he commanded the most mighty men that were in his army to bind Shadrach, Meshach, and Abed-nego, and to cast them into the burning fiery furnace. Then these men were bound in their coats, their hosen, and their hats, and their other garments, and were cast into the midst of the burning fiery furnace.

Therefore because the King's commandment was urgent, and the furnace exceeding hot, the flame of the fire slew those men that took up Shadrach, Meshach, and Abed-nego. And these three men, Shadrach, Meshach, and Abed-nego, fell down bound into the midst of the burning fiery furnace. Then Nebuchadnezzar the King was astonied, and rose up in haste, and spake, and said unto his counsellors, Did not we cast three men bound into the midst of the fire? They answered and said unto the King, true, O King. He answered and said, Lo, I see four men loose, walking in the midst of the fire, and the form of the fourth is like the Son of God.

Then Nebuchadnezzar came near to the mouth of the burning fiery furnace, and spake, and said, Shadrach, Meshach, and Abed-nego, ye servants of the most high God, come forth, and come hither.

Then Shadrach, Meshach, and Abed-nego, came forth of the midst of the fire. And the princes, governors, and captain, and the King's counsellors, being gathered together, saw these men, upon whose bodies the fire had no power, nor was an hair of their head singed, neither were their head singed, neither were their coats changed, nor the smell of fire had passed on them.

Then Nebuchadnezzar spake, and said, blessed be the God of Shadrach, Meshach, and Abed-nego, who hath sent angel, and delivered his servants that trusred in him, and have changed the King's word, and yielded their bodies, that they might not serve nor worship any god, except their own God. Therefore I make a decree, that every people, nation, and language, which speak any thing amiss against the God of Shadrach, Meshach, and Abed-nego, shall be cut in pieces, and their houses shall be made a dunghill: because there is no other God that can deliver after this sort. Then the King promoted Shadrach, Meshach, and Abed-nego, in the province of Babylon.

Two angels materialized themselves and went down to Sodom and Gomorrah to warn Lot to take his family out of town because a big disaster was going to happen. They also told Lot's wife that she was not to turn and look back at the city when they left, but she did not heed their warning and looked back. So she turned into a pillar of salt.

The same angels who spoke to these men of old who have transitioned so long ago are still with us today because angels do not die as humans do. They are spiritual beings, and Spirit does not die. We have been protected from so many unseen dangers and don't even know because we can only see material things. God has a limit on what we are supposed to see with our eyes for our own protection.

There are sixty-six books in the Bible, and angels are mentioned in thirty-four of them. Jesus said in Matthew 18:10, "Take heed that ye despise not one of these little ones; for I say unto you, that in heaven their angels do always behold the face of my Father which is in heaven." 1 Peter 1:12 tells us that angels do look into things on this earth. Angels take their command very seriously. They stand ready at all times to do the will of Jesus now in management because his Father put everything in his hands. Matthew 13:41–42 said, "The Son of man shall send forth his angels, and they shall gather out of his Kingdom all things that offend, and them which do iniquity; And shall cast them into a furnace of fire: there shall be wailing and gnashing of teeth."

So for all those that are still playing church, regroup before it's too late. Jesus knows the heart condition of every man, woman, boy, and girl. Remember always that only the child of God with a clean hand and pureness in their heart will see Jesus and his heavenly Father.

Our loving heavenly Father created us to worship him and be in constant communication with him through the connection of the spirits. Maybe we are not praying or communicating as much as we should. We need to follow Jesus's examples more closely because he talks to Father a lot when he was here in the flesh with us. We are here in the flesh, we thank God for the time he has given us to experience this part of his vast universe, and he wants us to live a good, healthy, and prosperous life while we are here on earth, but the better part of us is our spiritual side. The fleshly side of us tries to be more dominant and craves our attention to be directed toward our needs and desires. People of God, we have to establish a balance skillfully because we are encouraged to store up our treasures in heaven although we are living here on Earth. The life we are living here on this planet should be remembered as just a temporary vacation and not even a day in our heavenly Father's timing.

How wonderful and inspiring it is to know that we, the people of God, have so much love from our Creator, and wherever we are, even if we were abandoned in exiles as they did to the apostle John on the plains of Patmos, we know our heavenly host is there with us. Of course, at the time, they thought they were keeping him from the things of the flesh but not realizing that they were connecting him spiritually to where his heavenly Father needed him to be to work on the book of Revelation. If we stay committed and truly connected to God through his beloved Son, Jesus, we then attach ourselves and share in the apostle Paul's determination that there is nothing that this world can do to us that would separate us from the love of God.

Please read from Romans 8:37–39, "Nay, in all these things we are more than conquerors through him that loved us. For I am persuaded, that neither death, nor life, nor angels, nor principalities, nor powers, nor things present, nor things to come, Nor height, nor depth, nor any creature, shall be able to separate us from the love of God, which is in Christ Jesus our Lord.

Yes, my brothers and sisters, joining the army of the Lord is a lifetime commitment, and it is beautiful, just lovely. It will generate a warmness within that can get so hot as the prophet Jeremiah experienced that he declared it is like fire caught up in my bones. Do not be afraid to dance for the Lord when the Spirit hits you. You will move better than you did in the old life. Now you are dancing for the future of residing in everlasting life. Angels are dancing around the heavenly throne of God constantly to his glory, hallelujah to His name forever and ever.

Let it be known to Satan and his demonic forces in high places that we are no longer afraid of his madness because we know without a shadow of a doubt that the heavenly host is with us as we travel through these barren systems of heartache and travail. We are confident that our heavenly Father will save us and will always be there when we need his help. Call on the name of Jesus. That is what we love to do. Whenever you say "Jesus," we get the angel's attention. That is why King David was so confident in his words when he said,

"Thou I walk through the valley of the shadow of death I will fear no evil for thou art with me thy rod and thy staff shall comfort me all the days of my life."

Children of the Most High God, if you thought you were alone, then think again because you are not alone even when you feel you are by yourself because your physical eyes did not see anyone else. If God would open your spiritual eyes, you would leap for joy like an overjoyed person, so it is better that we don't see them, although we know they are here, there, and everywhere we are. Be humble. It is not good to touch what you cannot see. Like electricity, it will zap you. Never tempt the Spirit of God.

I beg of you, brothers and sisters, to heed the advice of Hebrews 13:1–2, "Let Brotherly love continue. Be not forgetful to entertain strangers: for thereby some have entertained angels unawares." I hope that from all the Bible evidence shown, it is more relaxing on the fact of the Bible that God truly loves us and the heavenly host is at his command and ready to serve him in every capacity. We are the ones who need to communicate more with our heavenly Father.

Let us visit Psalm 34:6–9.

> This poor man cried, and the Lord heard him, and saved him out of all his troubles. The angel of the Lord en-campeth round about them that fear him, and delivereth them. O taste and see that the Lord is good: blessed is the man that trusteth in him. O fear the Lord, ye his saints: for there is no want to them that fear him.

> As Christians, we depend on the Bible, the words of God, for all our spiritual sustenance. We, the followers of Jesus Christ, the Son of the Living God, build our faith in everything about Jesus. We love you, Lord.